COUNTRIES, REGIONAL STUDIES, TRADING BLOCKS, UNIONS, WORLD ORGANIZATIONS

GREECE: BACKGROUND, DEBT, AND CYPRUS ISSUES

COUNTRIES, REGIONAL STUDIES, TRADING BLOCKS, UNIONS, WORLD ORGANIZATIONS

Additional books in this series can be found on Nova's website under the Series tab.

Additional E-books in this series can be found on Nova's website under the E-books tab.

Countries, Regional Studies, Trading Blocks, Unions, World Organizations

Greece: Background, Debt, and Cyprus Issues

Brian D. Newmann
Editor

Nova Science Publishers, Inc.
New York

For permission to use material from this book please contact us:
Telephone 631-231-7269; Fax 631-231-8175
Web Site: http://www.novapublishers.com

LIBRARY OF CONGRESS CATALOGING-IN-PUBLICATION DATA
Greece : background, debt, and Cyprus issues / editor, Brian D. Newmann.
p. cm.
Includes bibliographical references and index.
ISBN 978-1-61728-866-1 (softcover)
1. Greece--Foreign relations--Cyprus. 2. Cyprus--Foreign relations--Greece. 3. Greece--Economic conditions--1974- 4. Greece--Economic policy--1974- 5. Debts, Public--Greece. 6. Greece--Politics and government--1974- I. Newmann, Brian D.
DF787.C93G74 2010
949.507'6--dc22
2010026097

Published by Nova Science Publishers, Inc. ✢ New York

CONTENTS

PREFACE

The Greek city-state of Athens is believed to have developed the first known democracy around 500 B.C. Modern Greece has been a democracy since the toppling of a military junta in 1974. Since then, the New Democracy (ND) party and the PanHellenic Socialist Movement (PASOK) have alternated leadership of the government. ND ruled from March 2004 until October 2009, when PASOK won national elections and a clear majority of the seats in parliament. PASOK's victory has been attributed to anti-ND public sentiment caused by the economic recession, corruption scandals, and law-and-order issues. On taking power, PASOK inherited a severe financial crisis; economic growth has contracted for three consecutive quarters in 2009, and the budget deficit is projected to be 12.7% of GDP and debt to be 125% of GDP in 2010. This book focuses on Greece's foreign policy; debit crisis, reunifying Cyprus; and relations with the U.S.

Chapter 1- The Greek city-state of Athens is believed to have developed the first known democracy around 500 B.C. Modern Greece has been a democracy since the toppling of a military junta in 1974. Since then, the New Democracy (ND) party and the PanHellenic Socialist Movement (PASOK) have alternated leadership of the government. ND ruled from March 2004 until October 4, 2009, when PASOK won national elections and a clear majority of the seats in parliament. PASOK's victory has been attributed to anti-ND public sentiment caused by the economic recession, corruption scandals, and law-and-order issues. On taking power, PASOK inherited a severe financial crisis: economic growth has contracted for three consecutive quarters in 2009, and the budget deficit is projected to be 12.7.% of gross domestic product (GDP) and debt to be 125% of GDP in 2010. Therefore, the economy is the dominating issue on the government's agenda.

The Greek government's foreign policy focuses on the European Union (EU), sometimes-strained relations with Turkey, reunifying Cyprus, resolving a dispute with Macedonia over its name, other Balkan issues, and sustaining good relations with the United States. Greece has assisted with the war on terrorism, but is not a member of the U.S.-led coalition in Iraq and has a limited presence with NATO in Afghanistan. See also CRS Report RL3 3497, *Cyprus: Status of U.N. Negotiations and Related Issues*, by Carol Migdalovitz.

Chapter 2- Over the past decade, Greece borrowed heavily in international capital markets to fund government budget and current account deficits. The reliance on financing from international capital markets left Greece highly vulnerable to shifts in investor confidence. Investors became jittery in October 2009, when the newly elected Greek government revised the estimate of the government budget deficit for 2009 from 6.7% of gross domestic product (GDP) to 12.7% of GDP. In April 2010, Eurostat, the European Union (EU)'s statistical agency, estimated Greece's deficit to be even higher, at 13.6% of GDP. Investors have become increasingly nervous about Greece's ability to repay its maturing debt obligations, estimated at €54 billion ($72.1 billion) for 2010. On April 23, 2010, the Greek government requested financial assistance from other European countries and the International Monetary Fund (IMF) to help cover its maturing debt obligations. This chapter analyses the Greek debt crisis and implications for the United States.

The debt crisis has both domestic and international causes. Domestically, analysts point to high government spending, weak revenue collection, and structural rigidities in Greece's economy. Internationally, observers argue that Greece's access to capital at low interest rates after adopting the euro and weak enforcement of EU rules concerning debt and deficit ceilings facilitated Greece's ability to accumulate high levels of external debt.

Chapter 3- Attempts to resolve the Cyprus problem and reunify the island have undergone various levels of negotiation for almost 40 years. Prospects for a settlement that would end the political division of Cyprus appear to have reached a stalemate and may now enter a period of retrenchment possibly dominated by harder-line views by both sides and more difficult negotiations.

Despite a positive and concerted effort over the past 18 months and through 60 meetings between Cypriot President Dimitris Christofias, a Greek Cypriot, and Turkish Cypriot leader Mehmet Ali Talat to reach some type of acceptable solution, time and politics appear to be no longer on either's side. On April 18, 2010, Turkish Cypriot leader Talat faces reelection as "president" of northern Cyprus; by all accounts by observers of the Cyprus issue, he could have a difficult time winning. Polls taken in late March show Talat at least 15 percentage points behind his rival. His likely successor, Dervis Eroglu of the National Unity Party (UBP), while insisting that negotiations would continue, appears to have taken a harder-line posture toward a negotiated settlement, and there are even some in his party who are advocating a permanently divided island and international recognition for the Turkish Republic of Northern Cyprus (TRNC).

Chapter 4- Cyprus has been divided since 1974. Greek Cypriots, 76% of the population, live in the southern two-thirds of the island and lead the internationally recognized Republic of Cyprus. Turkish Cypriots, 19% of the populace, live in the "Turkish Republic of Northern Cyprus" (TRNC), recognized only by Turkey, with about 36,000 Turkish troops providing security. United Nations peacekeeping forces (UNFICYP) maintain a buffer zone between the two. Since the late 1970s, the U.N., with U.S. support, has promoted negotiations aimed at reuniting the island as a federal, bicommunal, bizonal republic. The U.N. Secretary-General's April 5, 1992, "Set of Ideas" was a major, but unsuccessful, framework for negotiations for a settlement. Next, both sides accepted U.N. confidence-building measures only in principle and they were not recorded or implemented.

The prospect of Cyprus's European Union (EU) accession and its eventual membership intensified and complicated settlement efforts. On November 11, 2002, Secretary-General Kofi Annan submitted a comprehensive settlement Plan, but the two sides did not agree on it. After more negotiations, Annan announced on March 11, 2003 that his efforts had failed. Cyprus signed an accession treaty to join the EU on April 16.

The December 14, 2003, Turkish Cypriot parliamentary elections produced a new government determined to reach a settlement. After the U.N. led negotiations between the parties and with Greek and Turkish leaders present, Annan presented a final, revised Plan on March 31, 2004. In referenda on April 24, 76% of Greek Cypriot voters rejected the Plan, while 65% of Turkish Cypriot voters accepted it. Annan blamed President Tassos Papadopoulos, a Greek Cypriot, for the result. Cyprus joined the EU on May 1, 2004. More than two years later, Papadopoulos and Turkish Cypriot leader Mehmet Ali Talat agreed, on July 8, 2006, to discuss "issues that affect day-to-day life" and, concurrently, substantive issues. The accord was not implemented.

Dimitris Christofias's election as Cypriot president on February 24, 2008 ended the impasse. On March 21, he and Talat agreed to resume the settlement process, with working groups and technical committees. In September, they began direct negotiations for a solution to the Cyprus issue. Negotiations continue.

Some Members of Congress have urged the Administration to be more active, although they have not proposed an alternative to the U.N.-sponsored talks. After the 2004 referenda, the Administration worked to end the isolation of the Turkish Cypriots in order to diminish economic disparities between them and the Greek Cypriots and pave the way for reunification. Some Members questioned this policy. Members are maintaining their interest in Cyprus in the 111th Congress partly due to keen constituent concern.

Chapter 5- Let there be no doubt: Greece is a strategic Ally of the United States. As President Bush noted in his proclamation on Greek Independence Day last March, "Our two nations, were both born in the belief of liberty and self-determination, sharing common cultural bonds and national values. These bonds are strengthened by a mutual commitment to democracy and freedom worldwide."

Americans helped the Greeks to win their independence from the Ottoman Empire in 1821. Americans came to Greece's aid through the Marshall Plan from 1947 to 1948. We delivered invaluable political and military assistance to Greece's democratic forces during the Greek civil war. We have been a strong ally of Greece in NATO and have admired Greece's role in the EU during the last three decades. We have stood together in every major conflict of the last century, including the World Wars, the Cold War, and the crises in Bosnia, Kosovo, and Afghanistan.

These common values and beliefs are embodied by the millions of Americans who trace their ancestry to Greece, have enriched our own country and inextricably bind our two countries. The Greek-American community is the strongest and most durable bridge linking our two countries. Greek-Americans have established hundreds of fraternal organizations that provide support services and friendship to the Greek people. They have helped to stimulate trade, investment and two-way tourism. Our Greek-American community represents American values and interests in their interactions with the Greek people. Greek-Americans are invaluable to this relationship. I could not have done my job as Ambassador without them.

As members of the Trans-Atlantic community and as NATO Allies, we work together to advance shared interests in Europe and around the world. Whether working together to stem the tide of nuclear proliferation or the trafficking of persons and illicit materials, or to protect the environment, our shared interests bring us together time and time again.

Chapter 6- Greece has only minor domestic reserves of oil and gas and relies heavily on energy imports. In 2006, Greece consumed 1.4 Quadrillion Btu (Quad) of total energy of which 64 percent was petroleum followed by coal (23 percent), dry natural gas (8 percent) while hydroelectric and renewable energy combined accounted for 5 percent.

Oil consumption has increased in recent years, but has been outpaced by strong growth in demand for natural gas, driven by the development of new gas-fired power plants. The planned construction of a new oil pipeline from the Black Sea to Greece's Aegean Sea port of Alexandroupolis, the completion of a gas interconnector with Turkey, and the planned completion of a further gas link to Italy will establish the country as an important transit route for oil and gas supplies from the energy-rich Caspian Region to European markets.

In: Greece: Background, Debt, and Cyprus Issues ISBN: 978-1-61728-866-1
Editors: Brian D. Newmann

Chapter 1

GREECE UPDATE*

Carol Migdalovitz

SUMMARY

The Greek city-state of Athens is believed to have developed the first known democracy around 500 B.C. Modern Greece has been a democracy since the toppling of a military junta in 1974. Since then, the New Democracy (ND) party and the PanHellenic Socialist Movement (PASOK) have alternated leadership of the government. ND ruled from March 2004 until October 4, 2009, when PASOK won national elections and a clear majority of the seats in parliament. PASOK's victory has been attributed to anti-ND public sentiment caused by the economic recession, corruption scandals, and law-and-order issues. On taking power, PASOK inherited a severe financial crisis: economic growth has contracted for three consecutive quarters in 2009, and the budget deficit is projected to be 12.7.% of gross domestic product (GDP) and debt to be 125% of GDP in 2010. Therefore, the economy is the dominating issue on the government's agenda.

The Greek government's foreign policy focuses on the European Union (EU), sometimes-strained relations with Turkey, reunifying Cyprus, resolving a dispute with Macedonia over its name, other Balkan issues, and sustaining

---

* This is an edited, reformatted and augmented edition of a United States Congressional Research Service publication, Report RS21855, dated December 16, 2009.

good relations with the United States. Greece has assisted with the war on terrorism, but is not a member of the U.S.-led coalition in Iraq and has a limited presence with NATO in Afghanistan.

GOVERNMENT AND POLITICS

Introduction and Situation before October 2009 Elections

The Greek city-state of Athens is believed to have developed the first known democracy around 500 B.C. Modern Greece has been a democracy since the toppling of a military junta in 1974. Since then, two large parties have alternated leadership of the government: the New Democracy (ND) party and the PanHellenic Socialist Movement (PASOK). ND was in power from March 2004 until October 2009.In the September 2007 national elections, held after the government was criticized for poor performance in fighting widespread fires[1] and some officials were implicated in corruption scandals, ND was able to eke out only a slim majority of 152 seats in the unicameral 300-seat parliament. At the time, PASOK also suffered losses, while three small parties on the left and right registered significant gains and won seats. One of these, the ultra-nationalist, anti- immigrant Popular Reforming and Orthodox Rally (LAOS) party, entered parliament for the first time.

After the 2007 election, ND lost one seat in parliament and its position declined due partly to additional corruption scandals, a crisis of law and order, and the economic situation. An ongoing scandal over the Siemens Group's alleged bribery of politicians and officials sullied both major parties. Then, in September 2008, Merchant Marine Minister George Voulgarakis resigned amid allegations that government ministers had helped a monastery trade inexpensive land for prime real estate, at a cost of an estimated $130 million to the government. In October, the same scandal led to the resignation of State Minister and government spokesman Theodoros Roussopoulos, a close associate of then Prime Minister Constantine (Costas) Karamanlis.

Perhaps more significantly, the government's ability to ensure public security came into question. In December 2008, police fatally shot a teenage boy, provoking days of violent protests by anarchists, students, and labor groups in Athens and elsewhere. It was the worst rioting in years, and its duration generally was attributed to socioeconomic causes (i.e., the youths' joblessness and lack of hope), although a culture of impunity also was blamed.[2] Critics castigated the government for its passive response and slowness in reestablishing law and order.[3] In June 2009, the murder of a police officer who was a member of the counterterrorism squad protecting a witness in a trial involving a terrorist group again highlighted the government's deficiencies in this area.

PASOK polled ahead of ND in public opinion surveys throughout 2008 and 2009, and PASOK leader George Papandreou repeatedly called for early elections. PASOK came in first, and the LAOS registered striking gains in the European Parliament elections of June 2009.

In August, Greece again experienced terrible fires and, while they were not as severe as in 2007, some criticized the government for its alleged failure in the intervening years to improve fire protection or to establish better coordination of fire-fighting efforts.[4] The government blamed extremely strong winds for the destruction. Other observers said that the government had mobilized assistance from the European Union (EU) and from individual European governments.

October 4, 2009, Elections

The president is head of state, but the prime minister is head of government and exercises most powers. In February 2005, former Foreign Minister Karolos Papoulias, the ND consensus candidate and a founding member of the opposition PASOK, won the presidency with 279 out of 296 votes cast in parliament. His term expires in March 2010.

On September 3, 2009, Prime Minister Karamanlis called for early national elections because, he said, he wanted to avoid a protracted pre-election period. Parliamentary elections had been scheduled for September 2011 and now would take place on October 4, 2009. Karamanlis claimed that PASOK had "forced" the early election when it announced that it would not support President Papoulias for reelection. Without PASOK, Karamanlis 's ND party would not have sufficient votes in parliament to reelect the president and a national election would have been required in order to reconstitute parliament so that a new president could be elected. Thus, the election campaign would have lasted for at least six months.[5]

ND's election prospects were bleak from the outset of the campaign as the economy was experiencing a recession. At the same time, the European Commission estimated that Greece's 2009 budget deficit would be 8% of gross domestic product (GDP), well above the 3% ceiling that the EU mandates for members, and the national debt would be 110% of GDP.[6] (These estimates have since risen.) By October 24, Greece was supposed to present to the EU a package of measures aimed at restructuring its public finances and cutting its fiscal deficit to 3.7% by the end of 2009, which few considered feasible.

In addition, commentators and opposition politicians had criticized the government for what they claimed was its poor performance in fighting fires again in August. (However, others thought that the government had mobilized rapidly, but that extreme winds had affected the effectiveness of fire-fighting.) Critics also assailed the government for its failure to improve law and order in the face of domestic terrorism and anarchism.

To help Greece overcome its financial crisis, Prime Minister Karamanlis presented an economic plan on September 5. It called for cuts in public spending, freezing public-sector wages and pensions, combating tax evasion, and structural changes. Critics wondered why the party had not done all that in its six years in office, although its one-seat majority in parliament probably constrained boldness. The plan could not have appealed to voting public-sector workers and pensioners.

On September 12, PASOK leader Papandreou presented a program for his first 100 days in office, calling for boosting demand with pay increases above the rate of inflation, extra pay for lower incomes, protection of borrowers and households in debt, combating price increases in the market, freezing utility rates for one year, and passing tax reforms to promote redistribution of income. He also proposed increases in public investments, supporting employment by subsidizing social security contributions for new hires of unemployed persons, and increasing unemployment benefits. The PASOK stimulus plan had a price tag €3 billion or U.S.$4.38 billion. Papandreou said that he would fund it with better tax collection, with the EU's National Strategic Reference Framework (ESPA) cohesion policy funds, and public-sector real estate.

The smaller parties also presented their views. LAOS leader George Karatzaferis sounded nationalist and populist themes, calling for EU help in guarding Greece's borders against illegal immigrants, the establishment of a quota for immigrants, and stronger policies to combat "the Turkish threat." He attributed a large percentage of what he asserted was a rising crime rate to illegal immigrants.[7] Meanwhile, at the outset of the campaign, the Coalition of the Radical Left (SYRIZA) survived a leadership dispute with the main party in its alliance, the Coalition of the Left Movements and Ecology's

(Sinapismos/SYN). SYN President Alexis Tsipras demanded to lead both SYRIZA and SYN, but other parties in SYRIZA resisted, and some wanted the head of SYRIZA's parliamentary group and former head of SYN, Alekos Alavanos, to head the list. SYRIZA entered the elections without a leader at the head of its list and Alvanos did not run for parliament.

In the end, it was widely believed that Greeks voted against the ND government more than for PASOK.

Voter turnout was 70.92%, down slightly from 74.14% in 2007.

Karamanlis resigned as ND leader and assumed a seat as a Member of Parliament from Thessaloniki. His successor is former Culture Minister Antonis Samaras.

Table 1. Results of June 7, 2009, European Parliament Elections

Party	Percent of Votes
Pan-Hellenic Socialist Movement (PASOK)	36.65%
New Democracy (ND)	32.29%
Communist Party (KKE)	8.35%
Popular Reforming and Orthodox Rally (LAOS)	7.15%
Coalition of the Radical Left (SYRIZA)	4.7%
Greens	3.49%

Note: The Greens are not represented in the Greek parliament.

Table 2. Results of the October 4, 2009, National Elections

Party	Leader	% of Vote	Seats (Change)
PanHellenic Socialist Movement (PASOK)	George Papandreou	43.92	160 (+58)
New Democracy (ND)	Costas Karamanlis	33.48	91 (-61)
Communist Party (KKE)	Aleka Papariga	7.54	21(- 1)
Popular Reforming and Orthodox Rally (LAOS)	George Karatzaferis	5.63	15 (+5)
Coalition of the Radical Left (SYRIZA)	Alexis Tspiras	4.60	13 (- 1)
			300 (Total)

New Government

Table 3. Key Ministers

Portfolio	Minister
Prime Minister and Foreign Minister	George Papandreou
Vice President of the Government responsible for coordination of the Council for Foreign Affairs and Defense and the Economic and Social Council	Theodoros Pangalos
Minister of Finance	George Papaconstaninou
Minister of National Defense	Evangelos Venizelos
Minister of Economy, Competitiveness, and Shipping	Louka Katseli
Minister of Citizens' Protection	Mihalis Chrysohoidis
Minister of Environment, Energy, and Climate Change	Tina Birbili

Prime Minister Papandreou proposed a smaller cabinet, created the new post of Vice President, and reconfigured several ministries. The Ministry of Economy, Competitiveness, and Shipping has been created from some elements of the former Merchant Marine, Aegean, and Island Policy Ministry and others from the former Economy and Finance Ministry. The Ministry of Citizens' Protection took over responsibility for public order from the Interior Ministry along with parts of Merchant Marine Ministry's marine safety and other components.

ECONOMY

Greece has a mixed capitalist economy, with the public sector accounting for about 40% of the gross domestic product (GDP). In its first term, the ND government cut the budget deficit and taxes on corporations, and was able to raise tax revenues due to an average annual growth rate of 4% and a crackdown on tax evasion. Unemployment decreased at first, but 20% of the population remained below the poverty level.[8] ND also passed some social security reforms, despite political opposition and labor protests. The European Commission wants even more action in this area.

Greece sustained its growth due to booms in tourism and shipping. (Greece has the largest merchant marine in the world.) It also plans to ensure its own energy security as well as become a major "energy corridor" with the Turkish-Greece-Italy (TGI) natural gas pipeline, the Burgas (Bulgaria)-Alexandroupolis oil pipeline, the South Stream natural gas pipeline from Russia to Europe, and a gas pipeline between Greece and Bulgaria.

However, during the brief second ND term, Greece began experiencing the effects of the global financial crisis and recession, which hurt shipping and tourism among other key sectors. GDP has contracted for three consecutive quarters in 2009. Almost all industrial sectors have seen declines. Unemployment hit 9.6% in July and is expected to grow. Moreover, Greece is facing a crippling projected budget deficit of more than 12% of GDP and a debt in excess of 125% of GDP for 2010.[9] As of December 2009, the Finance Ministry stated that the debt was a record €300 billion (U.S.$442 billion). Credit rating agencies have downgraded the debt, meaning that it will be more difficult for Greece to find lenders and cost it more to borrow.

The Papandreou government expects to submit a revised Stability and Growth Program to the EU in January 2010, with measures to reduce spending, increase revenues, and resume growth. Its 2010 budget reduces operational expenditures by 10%, suspends public sector hiring except in "sensitive" sectors, and proposes economic reforms.

Basic Facts

Population: 10.7 million (2009 est.)

Gross Domestic Product Per Capita: $32,000 (2008 est.)

GDP Growth Rate: 2.9% (2008 est.)

Unemployment Rate: 9.6% (July 2009 est.)

Inflation Rate: 4.1% (2008 est.)

Exports: food and beverages, manufactured goods, petroleum products, chemicals, textiles

Export Partners: Italy, Germany, Bulgaria, Cyprus, United Kingdom

Imports: machinery, transport equipment, fuels, chemicals

Import Partners: Germany, Italy, China, France, Netherlands, Russia

Currency: euro

Source: CIA, *The World Factbook*, November 27, 2009, Greek National Statistical Service.

The economy benefits from Greece's membership in the EU and the euro zone. Greece received an estimated $8 billion annually from the EU between 2000 and 2006 and will receive another $24 billion for 2007-2013. Participation in the euro zone is believed responsible for controlling inflation.

TERRORISM

Greek authorities have worked to dismantle two main domestic terrorist groups, the Revolutionary Organization 17 November (17N) and Revolutionary Popular Struggle (ELA). The U.S. State Department lists 17N, which was responsible for the murders of five U.S. embassy employees in Athens, beginning with CIA station chief Richard Welch in 1975, as a Foreign Terrorist Organization (FTO).[10] Although arrests and convictions of 17N leaders and members have been made since 2002, retrials and acquittals have led to the release of some of those convicted. Neither 17N nor ELA has been active for several years. Possible copycats, successor groups, or renamed cells of the older groups such as Revolutionary Struggle (EA) and Popular Revolutionary Action (LED) are active, as are small anarchist and anti-globalization groups, which operate mainly in the Athens area. A January 12, 2007, rocket-propelled grenade attack on the U.S. Embassy in Athens caused no casualties and did little material damage. EA claimed responsibility. In 2009, attacks by Revolutionary Struggle have become more frequent. In September, it claimed responsibility for a car bomb attack at the Athens Stock Exchange that caused widespread damage and injured a security guard.

In June 2004, parliament passed a law to implement the common EU counterterrorism policy. In January 2006, Greece began using new, more secure passports with biometrics to comply with EU regulations and executing EU-wide arrest warrants. It also ratified the extradition agreement between the United States and EU. The Greek navy participates in Operation Active Endeavor, NATO's antiterrorism ship monitoring effort in the Mediterranean Sea.

FOREIGN POLICY

Greece is a member of the EU and NATO. In addition to participating in NATO's Operation Active Endeavor and the International Security Assistance

Force in Afghanistan, Greece also is engaged in EU missions such as the EU Military Force in Bosnia and Herzegovina (EUFOR— Operation ALTHEA) and the EU Rule of Law Mission in Kosovo (EULEX). It also has military observers as part of an Organization for Security and Cooperation in Europe (OSCE) force in Georgia and, in January 2009, Greece assumed the rotating presidency of that organization.

Cyprus

The Republic of Cyprus has been partitioned between the Greek Cypriot south and the Turkish Cypriot north since Turkish forces invaded in 1974 in response to a coup on the island backed by the Greek junta, which favored uniting Cyprus and Greece. Greece strongly supports its Greek Cypriot ethnic kin in their efforts to reunify the island. In November 2002, U.N. Secretary General Kofi Annan offered a draft settlement plan to unite Greek Cypriots and Turkish Cypriots in a loosely federated United Republic of Cyprus. Prime Minister Karamanlis cautiously stated on April 15, 2004, that the plan's "positive points can prove to be superior to the negative ones," adding that it was up to the Cypriots to decide and that Greece would support their decision.[11] On April 24, 2004, 76% of Greek Cypriots rejected the "Annan Plan," while 65% of Turkish Cypriots accepted it. The settlement process then stalemated. In July 2005, Turkey extended its customs union with the EU to all new members, including Cyprus, but did not recognize the Republic of Cyprus or open its ports to Greek Cypriot ships. Greece has seconded the Greek Cypriots' demand that Turkey recognize Cyprus *de jure* and fully implement the customs union. It welcomed the renewal of the settlement process in March 2008, and has supported Republic of Cyprus President Dimitris Christofias in his direct talks with Turkish Cypriot leader Mehmet Ali Talat, which have been conducted under U.N. auspices since September 2008.

Turkey

Greece secured its independence from the Ottoman Empire, the precursor of modern-day Turkey, in 1832. The two neighbors historically have had strained relations, but began a period of rapprochement in 1999. In order for Turkey to become a more stable and peaceful democracy, Athens supports

Turkey's full membership in the EU if it meets EU standards. Greece and Turkey share interests in regional peace, growing bilateral trade ($2.8 billion in 2008), a natural gas pipeline, and combating terrorism and illegal immigration. Greece is now the fourth-largest investor in Turkey. In 2006, the National Bank of Greece purchased Turkey's fifth-largest bank for $2 billion. Prime Minister Karamanlis visited Turkey in January 2008, becoming the first Greek prime minister to visit in almost 49 years.

However, a number of issues remain impediments to greater progress in normalizing bilateral relations. They include the unresolved Cyprus dispute, the failure of Ankara to authorize the reopening of the Greek Orthodox Theological Seminary on the Turkish island of Halki and its refusal to recognize the ecumenical (worldwide) status of the Greek Orthodox Patriarch whose seat is in Istanbul, and what some Greeks consider Turkey's suspicious advocacy and political support for Muslims of Turkish origin in Greek Thrace.

Sharp differences over Aegean Sea sovereignty issues produced major crises in 1987 and 1996 that appeared to bring the two neighbors to the brink of military conflict. In order to avoid similar developments in the future, Greece and Turkey have held more than 40 rounds of exploratory talks concerning disputes over air space, territorial seas, continental shelf, and related issues over several years. Both sides appear satisfied with continuing talks, which have produced neither resolution nor conflict. Greece did not take its disagreements with Turkey to the International Court of Justice (ICJ) in December 2004, as proposed at the 1999 EU summit in Helsinki which reaffirmed Turkey's candidacy for EU membership. Greece accepts the Court's jurisdiction, but Turkey does not. Greece officially recognizes only a dispute over the continental shelf and, in July 2009, its Foreign Ministry reiterated readiness to refer that one issue to the Court. Athens also wants Ankara to rescind a 1995 *casus belli* parliamentary authorization of any steps, including military ones, if Greece exercises a right to a 12-mile territorial sea as allowed under the Law of the Sea Treaty. Greece is a signatory of the Treaty; Turkey is not. In addition, Greece objects to Turkey's repeated infringements of Greece's claimed 10-mile air space over the Aegean and to Turkish commanders' references to (Greek) Aegean islands/islets not named in treaties as "gray zones" that must be demilitarized. Territorial disputes appear to be surfacing more frequently and serve to highlight the continuing lack of a solution. Some emanate from each country's desire to explore for oil.

On October 10, 2009, Prime Minister Papandreou, who had been one of the fathers of the Greek- Turkish rapprochement in 1999 when he was foreign minister along with the late Turkish Foreign Minister Ismail Cem, made a lightning visit to Istanbul for a meeting with fellow ministers from southeastern Europe. It was his first trip abroad taken in his capacity as foreign minister.

Macedonia

The former Yugoslav republic of Macedonia declared its independence in 1991. Its territory covers 39% of the historic region of Macedonia; the remaining 51% is in Greece and 9% is in Bulgaria. Macedonia asserts its right to use and be recognized by its constitutional name, the Republic of Macedonia. Greece objects, claiming that the name usurps Greece's heritage and conveys irredentist ambitions against Greece's largest province, also called "Macedonia," which borders the former Yugoslav republic. Due to Greek objections, Macedonia joined the U.N. in 1992 under the provisional name of The Former Yugoslav Republic of Macedonia (FYROM), which is how Greece refers to it.

In 1995, Athens and Skopje signed an interim agreement to normalize relations and settle all outstanding disputes except for the name, and Greece ended an 18-month long trade blockade of FYROM.[12] Since then, officials of both governments have met with the U.N. Secretary General's personal envoy, U.S. lawyer Matthew Nimetz, to discuss the name, but have not reached a mutually acceptable solution. Greek officials call for a compromise composite name with a clear geographic qualifier (e.g., Republic of Northern Macedonia) to be used internationally.[13] They reject the suggestion that one name be used solely in Greek-Macedonian bilateral relations and another internationally.

In April 2008, Greece, whose position is "no solution means no invitation" for Macedonia to join NATO and the EU, prevented NATO from reaching a consensus on extending an invitation to Macedonia to join the alliance because no solution to the name dispute had been found. Athens argued that, because of that situation, Macedonia had failed to meet what Greece said was the criterion of "good neighborliness" required of new NATO members. The international trend in name usage favors Macedonia, with 125 governments recognizing it as the Republic of Macedonia. The government of Macedonia has said that it would never renounce the achievement of this recognition.

Despite the name problem, Greece is the top investor in the FYROM and bilateral trade is strong. At the same time, however, Macedonian Prime

Minister Nikola Gruevski appeared to exacerbate bilateral relations with a spate of actions. In July 2008, he sent a letter to Prime Minister Karamanlis calling on him to recognize a "Macedonian minority" in Greece, with a basic right to be educated in its mother tongue (Macedonian).[14] Greece recognizes only a Muslim minority as called for in the 1923 Treaty of Lausanne and described the letter as "provocative." Foreign Minister Bakoyannis charged that Gruevski was "trying to deliberately undermine" the name negotiations by inserting onto the agenda an "alleged Macedonian minority," whose existence Greece does not recognize.[15] In his reply, Karamanlis declared, "There is no 'Macedonian' minority," and called on Gruevski to leave behind "nationalist formulas of a bygone era."[16] A month later, Gruevski wrote to the U.N. Secretary General and to Nimetz, requesting that recognition of the Macedonian Orthodox Church be included in the name discussions. Nimetz said, "We are dealing with the name of the country and (not) ... with the national or with other personal identities of people."[17] Finally, in November, Macedonia filed a complaint with the International Court of Justice (ICJ) charging that Greece had violated the 1995 Interim Accord because Article 11 obliged it not to object to Macedonia's application to international organizations of which Greece is a member (e.g., NATO). Greece said that it would respond with evidence that Skopje has failed to adhere to the 1995 agreement.

Prime Minister Papandreou agrees with Karamanlis 's position regarding the negotiations with the FYROM. Officials in the new government have said that the FYROM's entry into the EU is conditional on a solution to the name issue and, due to Greece's insistence, the EU has postponed a decision on Macedonia's candidacy. However, Papandreou does have sufficient political capital at this stage in his tenure to compromise on the issue should he wish to do so.

Other Regional Issues

Greeks and Serbs have particularly close ties based on their common Orthodox Christianity, their alliance during the 20th-century Balkan wars, and Greek empathy during the division of Yugoslavia. Greece hopes that Serbia and all of its Balkan neighbors eventually will become EU members in order to strengthen regional stability. Greece sought a U.N. Security Council-legitimized, mutually acceptable agreement on Kosovo to reassure Serbia and protect Kosovar Serbs.[18] Therefore, it opposed Kosovo's unilateral declaration of independence—perhaps also wary that it might set a precedent for northern Cyprus. Athens has a liaison office and not an embassy in Pristina, as it still does not recognize Kosovo's independence.

Greece sent a 20-member military team to join an OSCE observer force in Georgia in August 2008, in the aftermath of the Georgia-Russia conflict. Athens does not recognize the Russian- backed independence of the secessionist Georgian regions of South Ossetia and Abhazia. Greece's policies towards Kosovo, South Ossetia, and Abhazia, and to a great extent Cyprus, are consistent with its support for the inviolability of international borders.

Afghanistan

In response to domestic critics, the Papandreou government has defended Greece's participation in NATO's Afghan mission in terms of its own national interests: providing diplomatic prestige, proving Greece's reliability, and adding to Greece's effectiveness in managing its own national issues.[19] Yet, the government may find its ability to support even limited commitments for Afghanistan severely constrained due to the ongoing economic crisis.

Greece's participation in the NATO mission is limited. The European Council on Foreign Relations lists Greece among the countries that have "underperformed" in Afghanistan.[20] According to the *IISS Military Balance, 2009*, Greece has an engineering company of 137 soldiers and one C-130 Hercules transport aircraft in Afghanistan. Former Defense Minister Evangelos Meimarakis argued that Greece is unable to send more troops or equipment to Afghanistan because of its own defense commitments, which usually refers to confronting a perceived threat from fellow NATO member Turkey. In particular, Greece believes that it cannot redeploy aircraft and helicopters from the Aegean Sea, where it accuses Turkey of violating Greek airspace and territorial waters.

Perhaps as a gesture to President Obama at the beginning of his administration, on April 4, 2009, former Greek Prime Minister Costas Karamanlis restated plans that had already been in motion. A Greek mechanized company would assume command of Kabul International Airport in 2010, with a reinforced strength of 3 0-40 officers. Until then, seven Greek soldiers were to be sent to assist other international forces already at the airport. If and when the airport is transferred to the Afghans, the mechanized company would move to the western province of Herat under Italian command. Officials suggested that these forces then would be closer to combat because more armed clashes occur in Herat. A battalion specialized in bridge construction already had deployed. In addition, Greece would return a medical unit to the field and a special unit would deploy to Kabul to train Afghan police officers.[21] Former Defense Minister Meimarakis also said that Greece was willing to train Afghan soldiers in Greece. Soon after it took power, the Papandreou government modified these plans. In particular, it declared that forces based in Kabul would not relocate to an area of higher risk (e.g., Herat) as had been anticipated by its predecessor. However, two medical units probably would deploy.

On March 31, 2009, former Foreign Minister Dora Bakoyannis called for a more prominent civilian presence in Afghanistan to assist with education, culture, economic development, and agriculture. Greek non-governmental organizations are involved in such programs. On September 22, the Greek Ambassador to NATO presented €300,000 (approximately U.S.$43 8,000) to his Hungarian counterpart to support development projects being implemented by the Hungarian PRT in Baghlan province, including building an outpatient clinic and rebuilding and equipping a school. In 2007, Greece had donated €500,000 (approximately U.S.$700,000) to Hungary for similar purposes. Despite the financial constraints noted above, the Papandreou government may opt to continue to contribute some funds for Afghan reconstruction in order to ease pressure from NATO allies.

Relations with the United States

U.S.-Greek bilateral relations are good and are based on historical, political, cultural, military, economic, and personal ties. The active, well-organized Greek-American community advocates pro-Greek positions and seeks close U.S.-Greek ties. The State Department refers to Greece as a "strategic partner," and Greece and the United States share interests in stability in southeastern Europe. Since the 1960's, the United States has operated a Naval Support Activity for the United States and NATO at Souda Bay on the Greek island of Crete under the terms of a mutual defense cooperation agreement (MDCA). The activity is a tenant of the Hellenic Air Force and supports U.S. Sixth Fleet Aircraft, U.S. Navy Air Detachments deployed at Souda, and transient U.S. military aircraft. In addition, an estimated 430 U.S.

ships to visit the base annually for servicing. A NATO Missile Firing Installation, used for testing, is located nearby.

The Greek government responded to the September 11, 2001, terrorist attacks on the United States with strong political support, unimpeded U.S. and coalition use of Greek airspace, and military assets for counterterrorism. Like some other EU countries, Greece does not view the war in Iraq as part of the war against terror and is not part of the coalition there. It refused to participate in training the Iraqi army in either Iraq or Greece and, along with five other EU member countries, refused to allow its military personnel assigned to NATO's international command staff to join a senior officer training mission in Iraq. It did, however, send military personnel to train Iraqis at a camp in Bulgaria and 100 BMP- 1 armored personnel carriers to Iraq to help equip the Iraqi armed forces. It also contributed financially to the cost of training Iraqi police and provided Greek commercial ships to transport NATO military equipment to Iraq. In addition, Greece provided some humanitarian and development assistance to Iraq.

U.S. aid for Greece has not been a major element in the bilateral relationship since the 1990's. In response to the 2007 wildfires, the U.S. Agency for International Development Office of Foreign Disaster Assistance (OFDA) provided more than $600,000 in emergency aid and $1.35 million through agreements with the U.S. Forest Service to implement a technical assistance program through the remainder of 2007 and throughout 2008. In FY2008, Greece also received $443,000 in International Military Education and Training (IMET) funds. In FY2009, it is receiving an estimated $100,000 for IMET, and the Administration has requested $100,000 in IMET funds for Greece for FY2010.

The United States has encouraged the rapprochement between Greece and Turkey, believing that direct bilateral talks are the best route to normalized relations. Both Greece and Turkey participate in the U.S.-initiated Southeast Europe Brigade (SEEBRIG), a rapid-reaction force consisting of contingents from seven regional countries.

At the same time, there have been some tensions in U.S.-Greek relations. In November 2004, Greece responded with a demarche when the United States formally recognized the FYROM as the Republic of Macedonia. The State Department said that the decision was not directed against Greece but intended to bolster Macedonia's stability and ensure its path toward a multiethnic, democratic state within its existing borders.[22] President Bush added that the United States still would embrace any name that emerges from negotiations between Athens and Skopje. The Bush Administration supported the U.N.-

assisted negotiations. Because the United States strongly supports Macedonia's integration in the Euro-Atlantic community, it regretted Greece's lack of agreement to a NATO invitation to Macedonia because the name issue was unresolved. Then Assistant Secretary of State for European and Eurasian Affairs Daniel Fried stated that the Administration would even have accepted a NATO invitation to Macedonia as the FYROM.[23]

Greece is one of only a few remaining EU member states not part of the U.S. Visa Waiver Program (VWP), which allows short-term visitors to enter the United States without a visa.[24] Greece had failed to meet the eligibility criteria by the time the program was frozen after 9/11. After the Greek government began issuing the more secure passports in 2006, it made joining the VWP a high priority. The Department of Homeland Security is conducting a process to include Greece in the VWP. H.R. 2261, introduced on May 5, 2009, would designate Greece a program country for the purpose of the VWP. On June 16, 2009, Assistant Secretary of State for European and Eurasian Affairs Philip Gordon told the House Foreign Affairs Committee that he thought that the process was near an end.

Greece values its role as an international energy hub in order to guarantee its own energy security and to collect transit fees. Yet, the Bush Administration was concerned about planned Greek energy links to Russia (i.e., the Burgos-Alexandroupolis oil pipeline from Russia via Bulgaria to Greece and the South Stream natural gas pipeline from Russia, Bulgaria, and Greece to Italy and Austria). This was because the Administration thought that the pipelines would increase Greek dependence on Russia, which already supplies 80% of its natural gas, and undermine efforts to ensure Europe's energy security by diversifying sources from excess dependence on Russia. In line with this view, the Bush Administration welcomed plans for the Turkey-Greece-Italy (TGI) pipeline that will bypass Russia to supply Azerbaijani natural gas to Europe. The Obama Administration's Special Envoy for Eurasian Energy Richard Morningstar has said that the Administration is neither "for" nor "against" South Stream.[25]

Although official U.S.-Greek relations are generally cordial, there is a strong strain of anti- Americanism in Greece, stemming from U.S. support for the Greek military junta that ruled from 1967-1974 and perceptions of U.S. failure to prevent the Turkish invasion of/intervention in Cyprus in 1974, among other issues. Unsupported allegations of U.S. interference in domestic Greek political affairs surface regularly. Anti-American sentiment is manifest in periodic mass demonstrations mobilized by Communists, anarchists, unions, antiwar activists, and anti- globalization forces, whose influence is disproportionate to their numbers in society.

End Notes

[1]Jeffrey Stinson, Joanna Kakissis, "Deadly Fires Take Toll on Greece's Spirit," *USA Today*, August 31, 2007.

[2] Iason Athanasiadhis, in "An 'Ungovernable' Democracy?" *Toronto Star*, December 16, 2008, says that unemployment among university graduates under 30 is 28%. Also, Dr. Stathis Kalyvas presentation on The Greek Riots: A Political and Historical Analysis, at the Woodrow Wilson Center for International Scholars, January 22, 2009.

[3] For example, Takis Michas, "Greece is Burning," *Wall Street Journal*, December 12, 2008, and Rachel Donadio, Anthee Carassava, "A Revolt in Greece, or Just Poor Security? Sense of Government Neglect is Pervasive," *International Herald Tribune,* December 13, 2008. Some suggest that the "culture of impunity" followed the military junta's brutal crackdown of student protests at the National Polytechnic University in 1973. Later democratic governments have been reluctant to deploy even less forceful measures against demonstrators, and university campuses have become "no-go" zones for security forces.

[4] Anthee Carassava, "Anger Flares among Greeks as Fires Continue to Burn," *New York Times*, August 25, 2009.

[5] Parliament elects the president of Greece. To be elected, a candidate must secure 200 votes in a first or second round or 180 votes in a third round. If it cannot elect a president in the third round, parliament is dissolved and elections are called. In a new parliament, a candidate then needs 180 (out of 300) votes in a first round, 151 in a second round, or a plurality in a third round. PASOK sought early elections and, to get them, it withheld support for Papoulias, whom it would otherwise have favored. ND, with only 151 seats in parliament, would have fallen far sort of the needed 180 votes. After it took power, PASOK endorsed Papoulias's re-election and, with both major parties supporting him, parliament is expected to grant the President another term when it votes in March 2010.

[6] Anthee Carassava, "Greek Premier, Dogged by Many Troubles, Takes Risk with Snap Elections," *New York Times*, September 4, 2009.

[7] "Small Parties on Social Policy, Economy," ANA-MPA, September 21, 2009.

[8] Anthee Carassava, "Early Greek Election Keyed to Economy," *International Herald Tribune*, August 18, 2007.

[9] Andrew Willis, "EU Demands Greek action in Wake of Downgrade," *euobserver.com*, December 9, 2009, Open Source Center Document EUP20091209167015.

[10] U.S. State Department, *Country Reports on Terrorism 2008,* released on April 30, 2009..

[11] "Greek Prime Minister Announces Government Stand on Annan Plan, Cyprus," NET Television, April 4, 2004, Open Source Center Document GMP20040415000150.

[12] For text, see http://untreaty.un.org/unts/120001_144071/6/3/00004456.pdf.

[13] "Greek Government Faces Difficult Political Choices on Macedonia Naming Issue," *To Vima*, October 17, 2007, Open Source Center Document EUP20071021 143001.

[14] Text of letter, "Gruevski's Letter to Karamanlis – I Expect You to Take Measures in Amending Injustice Cause to Greek-Born Ethnic Macedonians" MIA (Skopje), July 14, 1008, Open Source Center Document EUP20080714107009.

[15] "FM on Gruevski Letter," ANA-MPA, July 15, 2009.

[16] Text of letter, "PM Karamanlis' Letter of Reply to FYROM Counterpart Released," ANA-MPA, July 18, 2008.

[17] P. Panagiotou, "Nimetz Statements on FYROM Name Issue," ANA-MPA, September 24, 2008.

[18] M. Aroni, "FM Bakoyannis Says Greece Will Decide at 'Later Stage' on Kosovo,'" ANA, February 18, 2008.

[19] Defense Minister Evangelos Venizelos, responding to a question in the Parliamentary Permanent Foreign Affairs and Defense Committee, November 25, 2009, "Greece Parliamentary Foreign Affairs-Defense Committee Holds 1st public Session," Open Source Center Document EUP20091 127431017.

[20] Daniel Korski, "Shaping Europe's Afghan Surge," *Policy Brief*, European Council on Foreign Relations, March 2009.

[21] Kira Adham, "A Consolation Hug from Obama," *Athens Enet*, April 6, 2009, Open Source Center Document EUP20090413143003.

[22] State Department spokesman Richard Boucher, quoted by Nicholas Wood, "U.S. Grants Macedonia Name Recognition it Wants," *International Herald Tribune*, November 5, 2004.

[23] Dhimitris Y. Apokis, "We Have Never Recognized a Macedonian Ethnicity or Language," *O Kosmos tou Ependhiti*, April 12, 2008, Open Source Center Document EUP20080417141001.

[24] For background, see CRS Report RL32221, *Visa Waiver Program*, by Alison Siskin.

[25] "Summit Urges Greater Cooperation, Diversification for Europe's Energy Security," Xinhua News Agency, April 27, 2009.

In: Greece: Background, Debt, and Cyprus Issues ISBN: 978-1-61728-866-1
Editors: Brian D. Newmann

Chapter 2

GREECE'S DEBT CRISIS: OVERVIEW, POLICY RESPONSES, AND IMPLICATIONS*

Rebecca M. Nelson, Paul Belkin and Derek E. Mix

SUMMARY

Over the past decade, Greece borrowed heavily in international capital markets to fund government budget and current account deficits. The reliance on financing from international capital markets left Greece highly vulnerable to shifts in investor confidence. Investors became jittery in October 2009, when the newly elected Greek government revised the estimate of the government budget deficit for 2009 from 6.7% of gross domestic product (GDP) to 12.7% of GDP. In April 2010, Eurostat, the European Union (EU)'s statistical agency, estimated Greece's deficit to be even higher, at 13.6% of GDP. Investors have become increasingly nervous about Greece's ability to repay its maturing debt obligations, estimated at €54 billion ($72.1 billion) for 2010. On April 23, 2010, the Greek government requested financial assistance from other European countries and the International Monetary Fund (IMF) to help cover its maturing debt obligations. This chapter analyses the Greek debt crisis and implications for the United States.

---

* This is an edited, reformatted and augmented edition of a United States Congressional Research Service publication, Report R41167, dated April 27, 2010.

The debt crisis has both domestic and international causes. Domestically, analysts point to high government spending, weak revenue collection, and structural rigidities in Greece's economy. Internationally, observers argue that Greece's access to capital at low interest rates after adopting the euro and weak enforcement of EU rules concerning debt and deficit ceilings facilitated Greece's ability to accumulate high levels of external debt.

During the crisis, the Greek government has sold bonds in order to raise needed funds. Greece's government has also unveiled, amidst domestic protests, austerity measures aimed at reducing the government deficit below 3% of GDP by 2012. It also appears likely that Greece will receive financial assistance from countries that use the euro as their national currency (the Eurozone) and the IMF in order to avoid defaulting on its debt. A common method for addressing budget and current account deficits, currency devaluation, is not possible for Greece as long as it uses the euro as its national currency. If the austerity measures and financial assistance from outside parties prove insufficient, Greece could be forced to default on, or restructure, its debt.

Greece's crisis has numerous broader policy implications. There is concern that Greece's crisis could spill over to other European countries in difficult economic positions, including Portugal, Ireland, Italy, and Spain. Greece's crisis has raised questions about imbalances within the Eurozone, which has a common monetary policy but diverse national fiscal policies. It has also come to light that complex financial instruments may have played a role in helping Greece accumulate and conceal its debt, which may have ramifications for debates in the United States and the EU over financial regulatory reform.

Greece's crisis could have several implications for the United States. First, falling investor confidence in the Eurozone could further weaken the euro and, in turn, widen the U.S. trade deficit. Second, given the strong economic ties between the United States and the EU, financial instability in the EU could impact the U.S. economy. Third, $14.1 billion of Greece's debt is held by U.S. creditors, and a Greek default would likely have ramifications for these creditors. Fourth, some point to similarities between the financial situation in Greece and the United States, implying that Greece's current crisis foreshadows what the United States could face in the future. Others argue that the analogy is weak, because the United States, unlike Greece, has a floating exchange rate and the dollar is a reserve currency. Fifth, the debate about imbalances within the Eurozone is similar to the debates about U.S.-China imbalances, and reiterates how, in a globalized economy, the economic policies of one country impact other countries' economies.

INTRODUCTION

Historically, financial crises have been followed by a wave of governments defaulting on their debt obligations.[1] Financial crises tend to lead to, or exacerbate, sharp economic downturns, low government revenues, widening government deficits, and high levels of debt, pushing many governments into default.[2] As recovery from the global financial crisis begins, but the global recession endures, some point to the threat of a second wave of the crisis: sovereign debt crises.[3]

Greece is currently facing a classic sovereign debt crisis. Greece accumulated high levels of debt during the decade before the crisis, when capital markets were highly liquid. As the crisis has unfolded, and capital markets have become more illiquid, Greece may no longer be able to roll over its maturing debt obligations. Some analysts have discussed the possibility of a Greek default. To avoid such a default, however, the Greek government has introduced a variety of austerity measures and, on April 23, 2010, formally requested financial assistance from the other 15 European Union (EU) member states that use the euro as their national currency (the Eurozone) and the International Monetary Fund (IMF).[4]

Greece's debt crisis has raised a host of questions about the merits of the euro and the prospects for future European integration, with some calling for more integration and others less. Some have also pointed to possible problems associated with a common monetary policy but diverse national fiscal policies. Finally, Greece's debt crisis has implications for the United States. The United States and the EU have exceptionally strong economic ties, and a crisis in Greece that threatens to spill over to other Southern European countries could impact U.S. economic relations with the EU.

Given this context, congressional interest in Greece's debt crisis is high. Numerous congressional hearings in 2010 have referenced Greece's economic situation, including hearings before the House Committees on Appropriations, the Budget, Financial Services, Foreign Affairs, and Select Intelligence; the Senate Committees on Finance and Banking, Housing, and Urban Affairs; and the Joint Committee on Economics. The House Committee on Financial Services has scheduled a hearing for April 29, 2010, on the implications of

Greece's debt crisis for credit default swaps. Finally, Greece's economic situation was a major focus of discussion during Greece Prime Minister George Papandreou's meetings with congressional leaders in a visit to Washington, DC, in March 2010.[5]

This chapter provides an overview of the crisis; outlines the major causes of the crisis, focusing on both domestic and international factors; examines how Greece, the Eurozone members, and the IMF have responded to the crisis; and highlights the broader implications of Greece's debt crisis, including for the United States.

GREECE'S DEBT CRISIS: BACKGROUND

Build-Up to the Current Crisis

During the decade preceding the global financial crisis that started in fall 2008, Greece's government borrowed heavily from abroad to fund substantial government budget and current account deficits.[6] Between 2001, when Greece adopted the euro as its currency, and 2008, Greece's reported budget deficits averaged 5% per year, compared to a Eurozone average of 2%, and current account deficits averaged 9% per year, compared to a Eurozone average of 1%.[7] In 2009, the budget deficit is estimated to have been more than 13% of GDP. Many attribute the budget and current account deficits to the high spending of successive Greek governments.[8]

Greece funded these twin deficits by borrowing in international capital markets, leaving it with a chronically high external debt (115% of GDP in 2009).[9] Both Greece's budget deficit and external debt level are well above those permitted by the rules governing the EU's Economic and Monetary Union (EMU). Specifically, the EU's Stability and Growth Pact calls for budget deficit ceilings of 3% of GDP and external debt ceilings of 60% of GDP. Greece is not alone, however, in exceeding these limits. Of the 27 EU member states, 20 currently exceed the deficit ceiling set out in the Stability and Growth Pact.[10]

Greece's reliance on external financing for funding budget and current account deficits left its economy highly vulnerable to shifts in investor confidence. Although the outbreak of the global financial crisis in fall 2008 led to a liquidity crisis for many countries, including several Central and Eastern European countries, the Greek government initially weathered the crisis relatively well and had been able to continue accessing new funds from international markets. That said, the global recession resulting from the financial crisis put strain on many governments' budgets, including Greece's, as spending increased and tax revenues weakened.[11]

Outbreak of the Current Crisis

Since late 2009, investor confidence in the Greek government has been rattled. In October 2009, the new socialist government, led by Prime Minister George Papandreou, revised the estimate of the government budget deficit for 2009, nearly doubling the existing estimate of 6.7% of GDP to 12.7% of GDP.[12] This was shortly followed by rating downgrades of Greek bonds by the three major credit rating agencies. In late November, questions about whether Dubai World, a state- controlled enterprise, would default on its debt raised additional concerns about the possibility of a cascade of sovereign defaults for governments under the strain of the financial crisis. Countries with large external debts, like Greece, were of particular concern for investors. Allegations that Greek governments had falsified statistics and attempted to obscure debt levels through complex financial instruments also contributed to a drop in investor confidence.[13] Before the crisis, Greek 10-year bond yields were 10 to 40 basis points above German 10-year bonds. With the crisis, this spread increased to 400 basis points in January 2010, which was at the time a record high. [14] High bond spreads indicate declining investor confidence in the Greek economy.

Despite increasing nervousness surrounding Greece's economy, the Greek government was able to successfully sell €8 billion ($10.6 billion) in bonds at the end of January 2010, €5 billion ($6.7 billion) at the end of March 2010, and €1.56 billion ($2.07 billion) in mid-April 2010, albeit at high interest rates.[15] However, Greece must borrow an additional €54 billion ($71.8 billion) to cover maturing debt and interest payments in 2010, and there are concerns about the government's ability to do so.[16]

At the end of March 2010, the Eurozone member states pledged to provide financial assistance to Greece in concert with the IMF, if necessary and if requested by Greece's government. In mid- April 2010, the details of the proposed financial assistance package for this year were released: a three-year loan worth €30 billion ($40 billion) at 5% interest rates, above what other Southern European countries borrow at, but below the rate currently charged by private investors on Greek bonds.[17] It is expected that an IMF stand-by arrangement, the IMF's standard loan for helping countries address balance of payments difficulties, valued at €15 billion ($20 billion) for this year would precede any assistance provided to Greece by the Eurozone members.

Investor jitteriness spiked again in April 2010, when Eurostat released its estimate of Greece's budget deficit. At 13.6% of GDP, Eurostat's estimate was almost a full percentage higher than the previous estimate released by the Greek government in October 2009.[18] This led to renewed questions about Greece's ability to repay its debts, with €8.5 billion ($11.1 billion) falling due in mid-May 2010. On April 23, 2010, the Greek government formally requested financial assistance from the IMF and other Eurozone countries. The European Commission, backed by Germany, requested that the details of Greece's budget cuts for 2010, 2011, and 2012 be released before providing the financial assistance. In late April 2010, the spread between Greek and German 10- year bonds reached a record high of 650 basis points,[19] and one of the major credit rating agencies, Moody's, downgraded Greece's bond rating.

Possible Causes of the Crisis

Greece's current economic problems have been caused by a mix of domestic and international factors. Domestically, high government spending, structural rigidities, tax evasion, and corruption have all contributed to Greece's accumulation of debt over the past decade. Internationally, the adoption of the euro and lax enforcement of EU rules aimed at limiting the accumulation of debt are also believed to have contributed to Greece's current crisis.

Domestic Factors

High Government Spending and Weak Government Revenues

Between 2001 and 2007, Greece's GDP grew at an average annual rate of 4.3%, compared to a Eurozone average of 3.1%.[20] High economic growth rates were driven primarily by increases in private consumption (largely fueled by easier access to credit) and public investment financed by the EU and the central government. Over the past six years, however, while the central government expenditures increased by 87%, revenues grew by only 31 %,[21] leading to budget deficits well above the EU's agreed-upon 3% of GDP threshold. Observers identify a large and inefficient public administration in Greece, costly pension and healthcare systems, tax evasion, and a general "absence of the will to maintain fiscal discipline"[22] as major factors behind Greece's deficit.

According to the OECD, as of 2004, spending on public administration as a percentage of total public expenditure in Greece was higher than in any other OECD member, "with no evidence that the quantity or quality of the services are superior."[23] In 2009, Greek government expenditures accounted for 50% of GDP.[24] Successive Greek governments have taken steps to modernize and consolidate the public administration. However, observers continue to cite over-staffing and poor productivity in the public sector as an impediment to improved economic performance. An aging Greek population—the percentage of Greeks aged over 64 is expected to rise from 19% in 2007 to 32% in 2060—could place additional burdens on public spending and what is widely considered one of Europe's most generous pension systems. According to the OECD, Greece's "replacement rate of 70%-80% of wages (plus any benefits from supplementary schemes) is high, and entitlement to a full pension requires only 35 years of contributions, compared to 40 in many other countries."[25] Absent reform, total Greek public pension payments are expected to increase from 11.5% of GDP in 2005 to 24% of GDP in 2050.

Weak revenue collection has also contributed to Greece's budget deficits. Many economists identify tax evasion and Greece's unrecorded economy as key factors behind the deficits. They argue that Greece must address these problems if it is to raise the revenues necessary to improve its fiscal position. Some studies have estimated the informal economy in Greece to represent between 25%-30% of GDP.[26] Observers offer a variety of explanations for the prevalence of tax evasion in Greece, including high levels of taxation and a complex tax code, excessive regulation, and inefficiency in the public sector. Like his predecessor Constantine (Costas) Karamanlis, Prime Minister Papandreou has committed to cracking down on tax and social security contribution evasion. Observers note, however, that past Greek governments have had, at best, mixed success seeing through similar initiatives.

Structural Policies and Declining International Competitiveness

Greek industry is suffering from declining international competitiveness. Economists cite high relative wages and low productivity as a primary factor. According to one study, wages in Greece have increased at a 5% annual rate since the country adopted the euro, about double the average rate in the

Eurozone as a whole. Over the same period, Greek exports to its major trading partners grew at 3.8% per year, only half the rate of those countries' imports from other trading partners.[27] Some observers argue that for Greece to boost its international competitiveness and reduce its current account deficit, it needs to increase its productivity, significantly cut wages, and increase savings. As discussed below, the Papandreou government has begun to curb public sector wages and hopes to increase Greek exports through investment in areas where the country has a comparative advantage. In the past, tourism and the shipping industry have been the Greek economy's strongest sectors.

International Factors

Increased Access to Capital at Low Interest Rates

Greece's adoption of the euro as its national currency in 2001 is seen by some as a contributing factor in Greece's buildup of debt. With the currency bloc anchored by economic heavyweights Germany and France, and a common monetary policy conservatively managed by the European Central Bank (ECB), investors have tended to view the reliability of euro member countries with a heightened degree of confidence. The perceptions of stability conferred by euro membership allowed Greece, as well as other Eurozone members, to borrow at a more favorable interest rate than would likely have been the case outside the EU, making it easier to finance the state budget and service existing debt. This benefit, however, may also have contributed to Greece's current debt problems: observers argue that access to artificially cheap credit allowed Greece to accumulate high levels of debt. Critics assert that if the market had discouraged excess borrowing by making debt financing more expensive, Greece would have been forced to come to terms earlier with the need for austerity and reform.

Issues with EU Rules Enforcement

The lack of enforcement of the Stability and Growth Pact is also seen as a contributing factor to Greece's high level of debt. In 1997, EU members adopted the Stability and Growth Pact, an agreement to enhance the surveillance and enforcement of the public finance rules set out in the 1992 Maastricht Treaty's "convergence criteria" for EMU. The rules call for budget deficits not to exceed 3% of GDP and debt not to exceed 60% of GDP. The Pact clarified and sped up the excessive deficit procedure to be applied to member states that surpassed the deficit limit. If the member state is deemed to have insufficiently complied with the corrective measures recommended by the European Commission and the Council of the European Union during the excessive deficit procedure, the process may ultimately result in a fine of as much as 0.5% of GDP.[28]

Following the launch of the euro, an increasing number of member states found it hard to comply with the limits set by the Pact. Since 2003, more than 30 excessive deficit procedures have been undertaken, with the EU reprimanding member states and pressuring them to tighten up their finances, or at least promise to do so. The EU, however, has never imposed a financial sanction against any member state for violating the deficit limit. The lack of enforcement of the Stability and Growth Pact is thought to have limited the role it can play in discouraging countries, like Greece, from running up high levels of debt.

The European Commission initiated an excessive deficit procedure against Greece in 2004 when Greece reported an upward revision of its 2003 budget deficit figure to 3.2% of GDP. In its report, the Commission indicated that "the quality of public data is not satisfactory," noting that the EU's statistical office, Eurostat, had not certified or had unilaterally amended data provided by the National Statistical Service of Greece since 2000.[29] Subsequent statistical revisions between 2004 and 2007 revealed that Greece had violated the 3% limit in every year since 2000, with its deficit topping out at 7.9% of GDP in 2004. The Commission also noted that Greece's debt had been above 100% of GDP since before Greece joined the euro, and that the statistical revisions had pushed the debt number up as well. The EU closed the excessive deficit procedure in 2007, with the Commission pronouncing itself satisfied that Greece had taken sufficient measures, "mainly of a permanent nature," and that the country's deficit would be 2.6% of GDP in 2006 and 2.4% in 2007.

The Commission also concluded that "the Greek statistical authorities improved their procedures," leading to "an overall higher quality of data."[30] The Commission opened a new excessive deficit procedure in 2009 when Greece's 2007 deficit was reported at 3.5% of GDP, and that procedure is ongoing in the context of the current situation.[31] This points to a broader problem of a monetary union without a fiscal union, as discussed below in "European Integration."

Addressing the Crisis: Progress to Date

In an effort to restore investor confidence in the Greek economy, the Papandreou government has pursued a series of wide-ranging fiscal austerity measures. However, the combination of spending cuts and tax increases do not appear to have appeased investors enough to enable Greece to raise the money it needs to cover its maturing debt payments. On April 23, 2010, Papandreou announced that Greece would draw on €45 billion ($60 billion) in emergency financial assistance from Eurozone members and the IMF in order to avoid defaulting on its debt obligations. Although European leaders and the IMF have welcomed the austerity measures taken by the Greek government thus far, they are expected to request additional measures and further details on plans to meet budget deficit targets in exchange for financial assistance.

Some have suggested that, in addition to austerity and financial assistance from Eurozone member states and the IMF, Greece could finance its budget deficit and increase the competitiveness of its exports by exiting the Eurozone and adopting and devaluing a new national currency. However, most consider this an unlikely policy course as both Greek and European leaders appear committed to ensuring that Greece remain a Eurozone member and exiting the Eurozone could make future borrowing costs much higher for Greece. If the government is not able to satisfactorily reduce its budget deficit through fiscal austerity or financial assistance from a third party, it may be forced to restructure or default on its debt obligations.

Greek Domestic Policy Responses

Fiscal Austerity

Since taking office in October 2009, the Papandreou government has unveiled three separate packages of fiscal austerity measures aimed at bringing Greece's government deficit down from an estimated 13.6% of GDP in 2009 to below 3% by 2012.[32] In total, the measures are worth an estimated €16 billion ($21.6 billion), or 6.4% of GDP.[33] The specific longer-term budget deficit targets established by the government are 8.7% of GDP in 2010; 5.6% of GDP in 2011; 2.8% of GDP in 2012; and 2% of GDP in 2013.[34] Greece's plan to achieve these targets is detailed in the country's Stability and Growth Programme, which was submitted to the European Commission (EC) on January 15, 2010, and approved by the EC on February 3, 2010; and in a follow-on report on implementation of the Programme submitted to the EC in March 2010.[35] Eurozone leaders have requested additional details on policy reforms for 2010, 2011, and 2012.

Eurozone member states have welcomed the Papandreou government's plans for fiscal consolidation and are expected to request additional measures be taken. Some observers express concern, however, that the mix of tax increases and sharp spending cuts could lead to higher unemployment and deepen an ongoing recession in the country. The policy solutions to two of the major economic issues facing the Greek government—cutting large government budget deficits (which requires contractionary fiscal policies to address) and stimulating the economy during cyclical economic downturn (which requires expansionary fiscal policies)—are at odds with each other. Some question, then, how long the government will be able to count on public support for the contractionary measures in the face of a sharp recession.[36]

On March 3, 2010, Prime Minister Papandreou won parliamentary approval for the third and most far-reaching of his government's proposed austerity measures. The package was widely considered an attempt to address concerns in other Eurozone member states that the previously adopted measures did not go far enough. A significant percentage of the additional revenues to be generated from Greece's previously announced austerity measures were projected to come from a crackdown on tax evasion and improved collection of social security contributions. Among other things, the March measures aim to increase revenue through a rise in the average value-added tax rate from 19% to 21%; tax increases on fuel, tobacco, liquor, and luxury products; and a one-off 1% tax increase on personal incomes of over €100,000 ($133,000). The government has also announced a series of corporate, personal, and real estate tax reforms. On the expenditure side, most of the spending cuts announced this year focus on the civil service. The measures include a civil servant hiring freeze in 2010 with a 5:1 retirement/recruitment ratio for new public sector hires from 2011; a 10% cut in civil service salary allowances (bonuses); a freeze on state pensions; and a 30% cut in public sector supplementary pay (equivalent to about one month of pay).[37]

Structural Reforms

Prime Minister Papandreou has repeatedly emphasized the need for longer-term structural reforms to the Greek economy. To this end, he has proposed wide-ranging reforms to the pension and health care systems and to Greece's public administration. His government has also announced measures to boost Greek economic competitiveness by enhancing employment and economic growth, fostering increased private sector development, and supporting research, technology, and innovation.

As mentioned above, the Greek pension system, considered one of the most generous in Europe, has long been a target of advocates of Greek economic reform. The Papandreou government has pledged both to reform pension institutions and to crack down on social security contribution evasion. At least one government official has been reported as saying that measures will include raising the average retirement age from 61 to 63 (the statutory retirement age in Greece is 65) and calculating pensions on the basis of lifetime contributions as opposed to the last five years of earnings, as is now the case with some civil service pension schemes.[38] Prime Minister Papandreou has announced a similar effort to tighten public regulation and strengthen accountability in what is widely considered an inefficient Greek health care system. His government also hopes to restructure Greece's public administration. This includes consolidating local governance structures by reducing the levels of local administrative authorities from five to three, reducing the number of Greek municipalities from 1,034 to 370, and reducing the legal public entities formed by local authorities from 6,000 to 2,000.

Some economists express concern that Greece's relatively drastic contractionary fiscal policies could hinder economic growth over the medium term. GDP contracted by 2% in 2009 and is forecasted to contract by 2.5% in 2010 and by 0.7% in 2011.[39] Registered unemployment reached 10.6% in November 2009, the highest level since March 2005, and is expected to increase in 2010. As of October 2009, 27.5% of young people (aged 15-24) in Greece were unemployed.[40] The Papandreou government hopes to counter these trends by attracting new foreign investment in Greece and by boosting exports of goods and services. In addition to advancing institutional reforms designed to more efficiently disburse Greek and EU investment and development funds, it intends to target sectors where it believes Greece has strong comparative advantages for trade and investment. These include its geographic location, particularly as a potential hub for regional trade and investment in energy and transportation networks; the renewable energy sector; and already strong global shipping and tourism sectors. Most agree, however, that the challenges to building sustainable economic growth are considerable. Greek exports dropped by close to 18% in 2009 and Greek businesses have become increasingly uncompetitive in domestic and international markets.[41]

Perhaps the most substantial challenge for the Papandreou government could be maintaining public and political support for its austerity and economic reform program. Papandreou's Panhellenic Socialist Movement (PASOK) came to office in October 2009 on a platform of "social protection" promising to boost wages, improve support for the poor, and promote redistribution of income. The policies he has since pursued to cut the budget deficit have required retreating from most of these campaign pledges, and could prove politically difficult to see through. Thus far, Papandreou appears to have maintained the support of the majority of Greeks. According to two separate February 2010 polls, 72% of Greeks support the Prime Minister and 65% of Greeks believe the austerity measures are overdue and necessary.[42] Nevertheless, thousands of public sector workers and their supporters have taken to the streets to protest the announced austerity measures, and more protests and strikes are scheduled. Observers expect heightened opposition should the government be asked to implement further cuts by Eurozone member states or the IMF as a condition for forthcoming financial assistance.

The largest opposition party, the center-right New Democracy (ND) unseated by PASOK in the 2009 elections, has thus far supported the fiscal consolidation measures taken by the Papandreou government. However, ND has criticized Papandreou's decision to call for IMF assistance, with ND party leader Antonis Samaras predicting that the "IMF is going to force new measures upon [Greece] that neither [the Greek] economy nor [Greek] society will be able to bear."[43] Long-time observers of Greece point out that the reform record of past Greek governments dating back to the 1980s is mixed at best. It remains to be seen whether the Papandreou government will maintain the public support and political will to see through its wide range of reform proposals.

Financial Assistance from the Eurozone Member States

On April 23, 2010, the Greek government formally requested the activation of a financial assistance mechanism that was formulated by Eurozone leaders during a series of meetings in March 2010 and early April 2010. The package could reportedly provide some €30 billion (approximately $40 billion) in bilateral loans from Eurozone countries this year, at an interest rate of about 5%, supplemented by an additional €15 billion (approximately $20 billion) from the IMF. Overall, the parties are reportedly discussing a three year deal (2010-2012) worth some €90 billion (approximately $121 billion) in loans. In order to complete activation of the mechanism, the European Commission and the European Central Bank must give a positive assessment of the Greek request and each Eurozone country would need to approve the agreement. While Germany is expected to give its assent in the end, the debate remains especially contentious in Berlin, where a parliamentary vote would be needed to approve the loan. Germany would reportedly provide the largest bilateral loan, expected to be about €8.4 billion (approximately $11.2 billion) this year, followed by France, which is expected to loan about €6.3 billion (approximately $8.4 billion). Ahead of an official decision, both of these countries have been pressuring Greece to lay out detailed deficit reduction measures for 2011 and 2012, indicating that their willingness to lend money is conditional on Greece sticking to a severe austerity plan.[44]

Debate leading up to the Eurozone pledge for financial assistance to Greece was contentious. Severe instability in the Greek economy, up to and including a default, could have considerable consequences for the EU, and especially the Eurozone. The crisis has contributed to a weakening of the euro's foreign exchange value, and some observers fear that a deepening crisis could spread across European bond markets and draw in countries such as Spain, Portugal, Italy, and Ireland. The cost of providing financial assistance to Greece is relatively low. Greece's total outstanding debt (approximately €300 billion, or $399 billion[45]) would add about 3% to the debt of the other Eurozone member states,[46] and it is unlikely that the full amount would need to be committed.

Beyond purely economic considerations, there is also a significant political element to the EU debate. Monetary union, and the hope that the euro becomes a reserve currency, is seen by many proponents of a strong EU as a crowning achievement of European integration. Some observers, therefore, assert that the EU must maintain solidarity above all else, arguing that EU members, and particularly the large countries of the Eurozone, must not allow Greece to default, much less abandon the euro.

At the same time, the debate has been a prolonged one because there is little political appetite in the EU for providing financial assistance to Greece. Most EU countries are themselves experiencing financial hardship, and many are exasperated by the idea of rescuing a member state that, in their perspective, has not exercised budget discipline, has failed to modernize its economy, and allegedly has falsified past financial statistics. In addition, many strongly wish to avoid setting a precedent by "bailing out" a member state that has not managed its finances well. Some observers have argued that allowing Greece to default is preferable to an EU rescue package. Germany, the Eurozone's largest economy and arguably its most influential national voice on economic policy, has been among the most skeptical member states. Polls show that a large majority of Germans are strongly against providing financial assistance to Greece,[47] and German Chancellor Angela Merkel repeatedly put a brake on EU discussions about formulating a rescue package for Greece before the final agreement was reached in March 2010.

Financial Assistance from the IMF

Greece has requested financial assistance from the IMF, expected to be worth €15 billion ($20 billion) this year. At the onset of the Greek crisis, many EU officials were insistent that the Eurozone take ownership of the issue. Analysts asserted that it was important for the Eurozone to demonstrate its strength and credibility by taking care of its own problems. "Outside" intervention from the IMF has been viewed by many as a potential "humiliation" for the Eurozone, with officials at the European Central Bank, among others, strongly opposed to the prospect.[48] In late March, however, the debate in Europe appeared to shift, with the door slowly opening for possible IMF involvement as a number of member states came to favor a twin-track approach combining Eurozone and IMF financial assistance.

In the end, IMF involvement was reportedly a key condition of Chancellor Merkel's willingness to compromise and agree to the "safety net" mechanism. Greek Prime Minister Papandreou had previously stated that Greece might turn to the IMF with a request for assistance if the EU failed to offer needed aid. Some economists have argued all along that the level of assistance that the IMF could provide to Greece, which is tied to member states' financial commitments to the IMF, would be too small on its own and should be part of a broader package of financial assistance provided by other Eurozone member states.[49]

Some argue that the policy reforms (conditionality) attached to an IMF loan would lend additional impetus to reform and provide both the Greek government and the EU with an outside scapegoat for pushing through politically unpopular reforms. The EU would also make policy reforms a condition of loans, but the IMF is seen as more independent than the EU and has more experience in resolving debt crises than the EU.[50] In addition to providing financial assistance, the IMF also stands ready to provide the Greek government with technical assistance in handling the crisis.

BROADER IMPLICATIONS OF GREECE'S CRISIS

Contagion

As mentioned, if Greece defaults, there is a risk of contagion to other Southern European countries, including Portugal, Ireland, Italy, and Spain (which, along with Greece, have been nicknamed the "PIIGS" or "GIIPS"). Like Greece, these countries borrowed heavily during the credit bubble before the current global financial crisis and have encountered investors who are increasingly nervous about the sustainability of their debt. Already, movements in the yields on Portugal's, Ireland's, Italy's, and Spain's bonds have closely followed Greece's.[51] Concerns about a spillover of Greece's crisis to its neighbors are rooted in memories of the Asian financial crisis in 1997-1998, where it is believed that investor herding behavior contributed to the spread of the crisis throughout the region. [52]

Some argue that there are important differences among the "PIIGS" that would make contagion from Greece to these other European countries unlikely. It has been argued, for example, that the low levels of national savings in Greece and Portugal put these countries in the weakest financial position, at 7.2% of GDP and 10.2% of GDP respectively, compared to an EU average of approximately 20%.[53] Spain and Ireland, by contrast, are closer to the EU average at 19% of GDP and 17% of GDP, respectively, putting them in a stronger financial position.[54] Additionally, Ireland has begun to implement far-reaching austerity measures that were passed by its parliament in December 2009.[55] IMF Managing Director Dominique Strauss-Kahn is reported to have downplayed the possibility of spillover from Greece to Spain or Portugal, suggesting that a crisis in Greece could be largely contained to that country.[56] Contagion is viewed as unlikely if the EU or IMF or both provide financial assistance to Greece.

Complex Financial Instruments and Financial Regulation

Through the crisis, it has been reported that Greek governments, underwritten by prominent financial institutions including Goldman Sachs, used complex financial instruments to conceal the true level of Greece's debt.[57] For example, the government of Papandreou's predecessor, Costas Karamanlis, is alleged to have exchanged future revenues from Greece's highways, airports, and lotteries for up-front cash payments from investors. Likewise, it is reported that the Greek government borrowed billions by trading currencies at favorable exchange rates. Because these transactions were technically considered currency swaps, not loans, they did not need to be reported by the Greek government under EU accounting rules. The Federal Reserve is currently investigating the role that Goldman Sachs and other U.S. financial institutions played in the buildup of Greece's debt.[58]

The role of complex financial instruments in Greece's debt crisis has exposed some tensions between the United States and the EU over financial regulation. Some European leaders have called for tighter financial regulation, including a prohibition on derivatives that are believed to have helped create Greece's debt crisis. Financial regulatory reform before Congress regulates, but does not ban, derivatives. In a mid-March 2010 visit to Washington, DC, Prime Minister Papandreou vocally criticized "unprincipled speculators" for "making billions every day by betting on a Greek default."[59]

European Integration

Greece's debt crisis has also launched a number of broader debates about the EU's monetary union. Since the introduction of the euro in 1999, skeptics have pointed to a mismatch between the EU's advanced economic and monetary union and an incomplete political union. Even within the economic areas, where the EU is more tightly integrated, the Eurozone has a single monetary policy but 16 separate (if loosely coordinated) national fiscal policies. Critics argue that this arrangement is prone to problems and imbalances that threaten the viability of having a common currency. Others assert that the Greek crisis points to the need for stronger EU economic governance, at the very least in the form of a tighter and more enforceable Stability and Growth Pact. Going further, some proponents of deeper integration would like to use the crisis to launch a discussion about moving towards a more integrated EU-wide fiscal policy.

Additionally, some officials and analysts have proposed that the EU create a new European Monetary Fund (EMF) that would allow it to respond more smoothly to financial crises within individual member states in the future, operating much like the IMF but on a regional, rather than global, basis. There is some discussion that this would require a new governing treaty for the EU, which may be politically difficult to pass. Following the Asian financial crisis in 1997-1998, similar proposals for creating an institution like the IMF, but operating specifically within the region, were discussed but no such institution was created.

Finally, Greece's crisis has brought to light imbalances within the Eurozone. Some Northern European countries, such as Germany, have relied on exports for economic growth and pursued policies that aim to promote such export-led growth, such as wage moderation to keep the costs of production low and make exports competitive. Combined with conservative fiscal policies that promote high levels of savings, these countries have run large current account surpluses. In contrast, some Southern European countries, like Greece, have had higher levels of wage growth and more expansionary fiscal policies, leading to less competitive exports and lower levels of savings. These countries have run large current account deficits and borrowed to finance these deficits.

Some argue that the Southern European countries now need to reduce their debt and increase savings, which translates to running current account surpluses.[60] Hopes for export-led growth may be difficult to realize, however, in the face of the global economic recession. Greece's reliance on tourism, which is highly affected by economic conditions (consumer spending on luxury items) and shipping, which is also affected by economic conditions (increased trade; low energy costs), raises real questions about trade providing much of a boost to the economy. Additionally, observers note that it is unclear whether the Northern European countries such as Germany are willing to take the steps necessary in their own domestic economies to reduce their levels of savings, curb exports, cut their current account surpluses, and promote this rebalancing within the Eurozone.[61] How imbalances will be resolved within the Eurozone may be an important component of debates about EU integration in the future.

U.S. Economy

In addition to shaping debates over regulatory reform, both between the United States and the EU as well as within the G-20 more broadly,[62] Greece's debt crisis could have at least five major implications for the United States. First, many expect that if investors lose confidence in the future of the Eurozone, and more current account adjustment is required for the Eurozone as a whole, the value of the euro will weaken.[63] A weaker euro would likely lower U.S. exports to the Eurozone and increase U.S. imports from the Eurozone, widening the U.S. trade deficit.[64]

Second, the United States has a large financial stake in the EU. The EU as a whole is the United States's biggest trading partner and hundreds of billions of dollars flow between the EU and the United States each year.[65] Widespread financial instability in the EU could impact trade and growth in the region, which in turn could impact the U.S. economy. On the other hand, instability in the EU may make the United States more attractive to investors and encourage capital flows to the United States. However, if the crisis is contained to Portugal, Ireland, Italy, Greece, and Spain, the effects on the United States would be smaller than instability throughout the EU as a whole.

Third, a Greek default could have implications for U.S. commercial interests. Although most of Greece's debt is held by Europeans (more than 80%), $14.1 billion of Greece's debt obligations are owed to creditors within the United States.[66] Although not an insignificant amount of money, the relative size of U.S. creditor exposure to Greek bonds however is likely too small to create significant effects on the U.S. economy overall if Greece were to default.

Fourth, the global recession has worsened the government budget position of a large number of countries. Some argue that credit markets may have awakened to the magnitude of the debt problem due to the large number of countries that are involved and the extent of the budget deficits. For example, some have argued that there are strong similarities between Greece's financial situation and the financial situation in the United States.[67] Like Greece, it is argued, the United States has been reliant on foreign investors to fund a large budget deficit, resulting in rising levels of external debt and vulnerability to a sudden reversal in investor confidence. Others point out that the United States, unlike Greece, has a floating exchange rate and its currency is a reserve currency, which alleviates many of the pressures associated with rising debt levels.

Fifth, debates over imbalances between current account deficit and current account surplus countries within the Eurozone are similar to the debates about imbalances between the United States and China. These debates reiterate how the economic policies of one country can affect other countries and the need for international economic cooperation and coordination to achieve international financial stability..

End Notes

[1] Jon Hilsenrath, "Q&A: Carmen Reinhart on Greece, U.S. Debt and Other 'Scary Scenarios'," *Wall Street Journal*, February 5, 2010.

[2] Carmen Reinhart, "The Economic and Fiscal Consequences of Financial Crises," VoxEU, January 26, 2009.

[3] For more on the global financial crisis, see CRS Report RL34742, *The Global Financial Crisis: Analysis and Policy Implications*, coordinated by Dick K. Nanto.

[4] The IMF is an international organization tasked with ensure international financial stability. It makes short-term loans to countries facing balance-of-payments problems.

[5] Kerin Hope, James Politi, and Anna Fifield, "G20 to Look at Monetary Fund Initiative," *Financial Times*, March 9, 2010.

[6] The current account is the difference between exports and imports, plus net income payments and net unilateral transfers. By accounting identity, the current account is equal to net inflows of foreign capital. Current account deficits are financed by foreign capital inflows.

[7] IMF, *World Economic Outlook*, October 2009 and European Commission, DG Economic and Financial Affairs, http://ec.europa.eu/economy_finance/publications/european_economy/public_finances_emu_en.htm.

[8] For example, see "A Very European Crisis," *Economist*, February 4, 2010.

[9] "Country Report: Greece," *Economist Intelligence Unit*, February 2010.

[10] Jacob Funk Kirkegaard, *Greece's Unlikely Disciplinarians: The European Commission and Europe's Bond Market Vigilantes*, Peterson Institute for International Economics, February 12, 2009, http://www.piie.com/realtime/?p=1185.

[11] For more about the effects of the global recession on government budgets, and how governments have tried to address these challenges, see CRS Report R41 122, *Limiting Central Government Budget Deficits: International Experiences*, by James K. Jackson.

[12] "Is Greece Heading for Default?," *Oxford Economics*, January 29, 2010.

[13] For example, see Kerin Hope, Quentin Peel, and Tony Barber, "Greece Turns on EU Critics," *Financial Times*, February 13, 2009 and Louise Story et al., "Wall St. Helped to Mask Debt Fueling Europe's Crisis," *New York Times*, February 14, 2009.

[14] "Fiscal Woes to Dog Greek Bonds Even if Aid Offered," *Reuters*, March 22, 2010.

[15] Exchange rate used in the memo is the exchange rate April 26, 2010: €1 = $1 .331. Source: European Central Bank, http://www.ecb.int/stats/exchange/eurofxref/html/eurofxref-graph-usd.en.html.

[16] Carrick Mollenkamp and Cassell Bryan-Low, "Greece Leaps One Key Hurdle," *Wall Street Journal*, March 5, 2010.

[17] Charles Forelle and Marcus Walker, "Europe Bankrolls Greece," *Wall Street Journal*, April 12, 2010.

[18] Peter Garnham, "Greece Crisis Takes Toll on Euro," *Financial Times*, April 24, 2010.

[19] Elena Becatoros and Melissa Eddy, "Greece Still Under Siege Despite Aid Pledge," *WTOP*, April 26, 2010.

[20] At constant prices. IMF, *World Economic Outlook*, October 2009.

[21] *Update of the Hellenic Stability and Growth Programme*, Greek Ministry of Finance, January 2010, http://www.mnec.gr/export/sites/mnec/en/economics/growth_programme_2005-8/2010_01_15_SGP.pdf.

[22] Ibid.

[23] Administration encompasses public services including: executive and legislative organs; financial and fiscal affairs; external affairs; foreign economic aid; general services; basic research; research and development; public debt transactions and other general services. "OECD Economic Survey: Greece," *OECD*, May 2007.

[24] Ibid.

[25] "OECD Economic Survey: Greece," *OECD* July 2009.

[26] "Country Report: Greece," *Economist Intelligence Unit*, March 2009; OECD Economic Survey: Greece, July 2009; and Hellenic Foundation for Foreign and European Policy (ELIAMEP), *Economic Fact Sheet Greece 2009/10*, March 2010.

[27] "Is Greece Headed for Default?," *Oxford Economics*, January 29, 2010.

[28] *Resolution of the European Council on the Stability and Growth Pact*, Amsterdam, June 19, 1997, *Council Regulation (EC) 1466/97*, and *Council Regulation (EC) 1467/97*, http://ec.europa.eu/economy_finance/sgp/legal_texts/index_en.htm.

[29] European Commission, *Report from the Commission: Greece*, Brussels, May 19, 2004, http://ec.europa.eu/economy_finance/sgp/pdf/30_edps/104-03/2004-05-19_el_104-3_en.pdf.

[30] European Commission, *Recommendation for a Council Decision Abrogating Decision 2004/91 7/EC 9 on the Existence of an Excessive Deficit in Greece*, Brussels, May 16, 2007, http://ec.europa.eu/economy_finance/sgp/pdf/30_edps/104-12_commission/2007-05-16_el_104- 12_commission_en.pdf.

[31] European Commission, DG Economic and Financial Affairs, *Stability and Growth Pact, Country-specific procedures*, http://ec.europa.eu/economy_finance/sgp/deficit/countries/greece_en.htm.

[32] On April 22, 2010, the EU's statistical authority, Eurostat, estimated the Greek government's 2009 budget deficit as 13.6% of GDP, higher than previously estimated by the Greek government. "EU Sees Wider Greek Deficit, Roiling Markets," *Wall Street Journal*, April 23, 2010.

[33] "Greece Economy: An Austere Future," *Economist Intelligence Unit*, March 9, 2010.

[34] Greek Ministry of Finance, *Update of the Hellenic Stability and Growth Programme*, January 2010. http://www.mnec.gr/en/economics/growth_programme_2005-8/.

[35] Greek Ministry of Finance, *Update of the Hellenic Stability and Growth Programme*, January 2010; and *Report to the Implementation of the Hellenic Stability and Growth Programme and Additional Measures*, March 2010. Both available at http://www.mnec.gr/en/economics/growth_programme_2005-8/.

[36] "Greece Economy: An Austere Future," *Economist Intelligence Unit*, March 9, 2010.

[37] For more details on the Greek government's proposed austerity measures, see Greek Ministry of Finance, *Update of the Hellenic Stability and Growth Programme*, January 2010; and *Report to the Implementation of the Hellenic Stability and Growth Programme and Additional Measures*, March 2010. Both available at http://www.mnec.gr/en/ economics/growth_programme_2005-8/.

[38] "Greece/EU: Athens Frets under Financial Supervision," *Oxford Analytica*, February 17, 2010. A 2008 reform of the Greek pension system legally reduced the number of pension funds from 133 to 13 (with five basic funds and eight smaller and supplementary funds). However, some observers have noted that the 2008 reforms have yet to be fully implemented.

[39] "Country Report: Greece," *Economist Intelligence Unit*, March 2010.

[40] Hellenic Foundation for Foreign and European Policy (ELIAMEP), *Economic Fact Sheet Greece 2009/10*, March 2010; "Is Greece Heading for Default?," *Oxford Economics*, January 29, 2010.

[41] Hellenic Foundation for Foreign and European Policy (ELIAMEP), *Economic Fact Sheet Greece 2009/10*, March 2010.

[42] "Greece Economy: An Austere Future," *Economist Intelligence Unit*, March 9, 2010.

[43] "Athens Upbeat After Aid Talks with IMF Chief," ekathimerini.com, April 26, 2010.

[44] Andrew Willis, "Germany, France press Greece over austerity measures" and "Germany underlines European credentials in Greek bail-out debate," euobserver.com, April 26, 2010.

[45] "Is Greece Heading for Default?," *Oxford Economics*, January 29, 2010.

[46] Paul De Grauwe, "Crisis in the Eurozone and How to Deal with It," *CEPS Policy Brief No. 204*, February 2010.

[47] Ralph Atkins and Quentin Peel, "Germans Oppose Greek Aid, Poll Shows," *Financial Times*, March 21, 2010.

[48] "Rebuilding Greece's Finances," *Economist*, February 4, 2010.

[49] Tony Barber, "Brussels Urges EU to Reach Greek Deal," *CNN*, March 19, 2010.

[50] "Rebuilding Greece's Finances," *Economist*, February 4, 2010.

[51] E.g., see Daniel Gros, "Greek Burdens Ensure Some Pigs Won't Fly," *Financial Times*, January 28, 2010; and Abigail Moses, "Greek Contagion Concern Spurs Sovereign Default Risk to Record," *Bloomberg*, April 26, 2010.

[52] Saleheen Khana and Kwang Woo (Ken) Park, "Contagion in the Stock Markets: The Asian Financial Crisis Revisited," *Journal of Asian Economics*, vol. 20, no. 5 (September 2009), pp. 56 1-569.

[53] Daniel Gros, "Greek Burdens Ensure Some Pigs Won't Fly," *Financial Times*, January 28, 2010. Italy is not discussed in this article.

[54] Ibid.

[55] "Country Report: Ireland," *Economist Intelligence Unit*, February 2010.

[56] "Greek Woes 'Unlikely to Spread'," *BBC News*, March 8, 2010.

[57] Louise Story, Landon Thomas Jr., and Nelson D. Schwartz, "Wall St. Helped Mask Debt Fuelling Europe's Crisis," *New York Times*, February 14, 2010.

[58] Nelson D. Schwartz and Sewell Chan, "In Greece's Crisis, Fed Studies Wall St.'s Activities," *New York Times*, February 25, 2010.

[59] George A. Papendreou, *Remarks on Rising to the Challenge of Change: Greece, Europe, and the United States*, Brookings, March 8, 2010, http://www.brookings.edu/~/media/Files/events/2010/0308_greece/20100308_greece.pdf.

[60] Philip Whyte, "Why Christine Lagarde is Right About Germany," *Centre for European Reform*, March 26, 2010.

[61] Ibid.

[62] The G-20 is a forum for discussing economic policies among 20 major advanced and emerging-market countries. Following the financial crisis, financial regulation has been a major topic of focus at the G-20 meetings. For more on the G-20, see CRS Report R40977, *The G-20 and International Economic Cooperation: Background and Implications for Congress*, by Rebecca M. Nelson.

[63] Wolfgang Münchau, "Why the Euro will Continue to Weaken," *Financial Times*, March 7, 2010.

[64] This effect was highlighted by Greece's Prime Minister in remarks at Brookings. See George A. Papandreou, *Rising to the Challenge of Change: Greece, Europe and the United States*, Brookings, March 8, 2010, http://www.brookings.edu/~/media/Files/events/2010/0308_greece/20100308_greece_papandreou_remarks.pdf.

[65] For more on U.S.-EU economic ties, see CRS Report RL30608, *EU-U.S. Economic Ties: Framework, Scope, and Magnitude*, by William H. Cooper.

[66] "Is Greece Heading for Default?," *Oxford Economics*, January 29, 2010.

[67] For example, see Patrice Hill, "Bernanke Delivers Blunt Warning on U.S. Debt," *Washington Times*, February 25, 2010, and Anne Applebaum, "America's Debt Spiral Resembles Greece's Crisis," *Washington Post*, February 17, 2010.

In: Greece: Background, Debt, and Cyprus Issues ISBN: 978-1-61728-866-1
Editors: Brian D. Newmann © 2010 Nova Science Publishers, Inc.

Chapter 3

CYPRUS: REUNIFICATION PROVING ELUSIVE*

Vincent Morelli

SUMMARY

Attempts to resolve the Cyprus problem and reunify the island have undergone various levels of negotiation for almost 40 years. Prospects for a settlement that would end the political division of Cyprus appear to have reached a stalemate and may now enter a period of retrenchment possibly dominated by harder-line views by both sides and more difficult negotiations.

Despite a positive and concerted effort over the past 18 months and through 60 meetings between Cypriot President Dimitris Christofias, a Greek Cypriot, and Turkish Cypriot leader Mehmet Ali Talat to reach some type of acceptable solution, time and politics appear to be no longer on either's side. On April 18, 2010, Turkish Cypriot leader Talat faces reelection as "president" of northern Cyprus; by all accounts by observers of the Cyprus issue, he could have a difficult time winning. Polls taken in late March show Talat at least 15 percentage points behind his rival. His likely successor, Dervis Eroglu of the National Unity Party (UBP), while insisting that negotiations would continue,

---

* This is an edited, reformatted and augmented edition of a United States Congressional Research Service publication, Report R41136, dated April 1, 2010.

appears to have taken a harder-line posture toward a negotiated settlement, and there are even some in his party who are advocating a permanently divided island and international recognition for the Turkish Republic of Northern Cyprus (TRNC).

For his part, Republic of Cyprus President Christofias has recently experienced his own internal political difficulties as one of his governing coalition partners, the Socialist Party (EDEK), quit the governing coalition on February 9, 2010, reportedly over disagreements with the President's negotiating strategy. Almost immediately following the EDEK decision, hard-liners in the other coalition partner, the Democratic Party (DIKO), forced a vote of the party's central committee on whether to abandon the coalition as well. DIKO hard-liners had also criticized Christofias for what they considered to be too many concessions to the Turkish Cypriot side. In the end, DIKO voted to remain in the coalition, but the outcome of both votes seemed to indicate that Christofias was no longer guaranteed support for whatever negotiated solution he could have achieved in the near term.

Despite these political setbacks, and although both sides appeared to remain far apart on the most critical issues for any settlement, both Christofias and Talat pledged to continue the negotiations right through the end of March. With the last formal negotiating session on March 30, Talat left the negotiations in order to step up his political campaign in a final attempt to win reelection. Some observers were hoping that at the last negotiating session a joint statement would have been issued by both sides outlining the extent to which progress has been achieved on the major issues under consideration. And, while both sides did issue a statement at the conclusion of the session, it did not contain any details or outline of the "important progress" both sides continue to refer to.

The United States has long maintained a position of strong support for a negotiated settlement. This has been reaffirmed by the Obama Administration. Many Members of Congress have continued to maintain their interest in Cyprus during the 111th Congress, partly due to keen constituent concern. Hearings could be anticipated on the future of the negotiations in the aftermath of the April elections in northern Cyprus.

BACKGROUND[1]

The island Republic of Cyprus gained its independence from Great Britain in 1960. Of the estimated 780,000 Cypriots living on the island, approximately 77% are of Greek ethnic origin, and roughly 18% of Turkish ethnic origin. (Maronite Christians, Armenians, and others constitute the remainder.) At independence, the Republic's constitution defined elaborate power-sharing arrangements between the two main groups. It required a Greek Cypriot president and a Turkish Cypriot vice president, each elected by his own community. Simultaneously, a Treaty of Guarantee signed by Britain, Greece, and Turkey ensured the new Republic's territorial integrity, and a Treaty of Alliance among the Republic, Greece, and Turkey provided for Greek and Turkish soldiers to help defend the island. However, at that time, the two major communities aspired to different futures for Cyprus: most Greek Cypriots favored union of the entire island with Greece (*enosis*), while Turkish Cypriots preferred to partition the island (*taksim*) and possibly unite the Turkish Cypriot zone with Turkey.

Cyprus's success as a stable, new republic lasted from 1960-1963. After President (and Greek Orthodox Archbishop) Makarios III proposed constitutional modifications in favor of the majority Greek Cypriot community in 1963, relations between the two communities deteriorated, with Turkish Cypriots increasingly consolidating into enclaves in larger towns for safety. In 1964, Turkish Cypriots withdrew from most national institutions and began to administer their own affairs. Intercommunal violence occurred in 1963-1964, and again in 1967. On both occasions, outside mediation and pressure, including by the United States, appeared to prevent Turkey from intervening militarily on behalf of the Turkish Cypriots. On March 4, 1964, the United Nations authorized the establishment of the United Nations Peacekeeping Force in Cyprus (UNFICYP) to control the violence and act as a buffer between the two communities. It became operational on March 27, 1964, and still carries out its mission today.

In 1974, the military junta in Athens supported a coup against President Makarios, replacing him with a more hard-line supporter of *enosis*. In July 1974, Turkey, citing the 1960 Treaty of Guarantee as a legal basis for its move, deployed its military forces in two separate actions to the island, and by August 25, 1974, had taken control of more than one-third of the island. This military intervention[2] had many ramifications. Foremost was the widespread dislocation of both the Greek and Turkish Cypriot population and related governance, refugee, and property problems.

After the conflict subsided and a fragile peace took root, Turkish Cypriots pursued a solution to the conflict that would keep the two communities separate in two sovereign states or two states in a loose confederation. In February 1975, the Turkish Cypriots declared their government the "Turkish Federated State of Cyprus" (TFSC). In 1983, Turkish Cypriot leader Rauf Denktash declared the "Turkish Republic of Northern Cyprus" (TRNC)—a move considered by some to be a unilateral declaration of independence. At the time, Denktash argued that creation of an independent state was a necessary precondition for a federation with the Greek Cypriots. However, he ruled out a merger with Turkey and pledged cooperation with United Nations-brokered settlement efforts. Twenty-seven years later, only Turkey has recognized the TRNC.

Between 1974 and 2002, there were numerous, unsuccessful rounds of U.N.-sponsored direct and indirect negotiations to achieve a settlement. Negotiations focused on reconciling the two sides' interests and reestablishing a central government. They foundered on definitions of goals and ways to implement a federal solution. Turkish Cypriots emphasized bizonality and the political equality of the two communities, preferring two nearly autonomous societies with limited contact. Greek Cypriots emphasized the freedoms of movement, property, and settlement throughout the island. The two parties also differed on the means of achieving a federation: Greek Cypriots wanted their internationally recognized national government to devolve power to the Turkish Cypriots, who would then join a Cypriot republic. For the Turkish Cypriots, two entities would join, for the first time, in a new federation. These differences in views also affected the resolution of issues such as property claims, citizenship of Turkish settlers who had come to the island, and other legal issues.

Annan Plan

Negotiations for a final solution to the Cyprus issue appeared to take a dramatic and positive step forward when on November 11, 2002, then-U.N. Secretary-General Kofi Annan presented a draft of The Basis for Agreement on a Comprehensive Settlement of the Cyprus Problem, commonly referred to as the Annan Plan. The plan called for, among many provisions, a "common state" government with a single international legal personality that would participate in foreign and EU relations. Two politically equal component states would address much of the daily responsibilities of government in their respective communities. The Annan Plan was a comprehensive approach, and of necessity addressed highly controversial issues for both sides.

Over the course of the next 16 months, difficult negotiations ensued. Turkish Cypriot leader Denktash was replaced as chief negotiator by a more pro-settlement figure, and newly elected "prime minister," Mehmet Ali Talat. Greek Cypriot President Glafkos Clerides was replaced through an election with, according to some observers, a more skeptical President, Tassos Papadopoulos. The Annan Plan itself was revised several times in an attempt to effect compromises demanded by both sides. Complicating the matter even more, on April 16, 2003, the Republic of Cyprus signed an accession treaty with the European Union to become a member of the EU on May 1, 2004, whether or not there was a settlement and a reunited Cyprus.

Finally, after numerous meetings and negotiations and despite a lack of a firm agreement but sensing that further negotiations would produce little else, on March 29, 2004, Secretary General Annan released his "final revised plan" and announced that the Plan would be put to referenda simultaneously in both north and south Cyprus on April 24, 2004. The Turkish Cypriot leadership split, with Denktash urging rejection and Talat urging support. Greek President Papadopoulos, to the dismay of the U.N., EU, and United States, but for reasons he argued were legitimate concerns of the Greek Cypriot community, urged the Greek Cypriots to reject the referenda. On April 24, what remaining hope existed for a solution to the crisis on Cyprus was dashed as 76% of Greek Cypriot voters rejected the Plan, while 65% of Turkish Cypriot voters accepted it. In his May 28, 2004, report following the vote, Annan said that "the Greek Cypriots' vote must be respected, but they need to demonstrate willingness to resolve the Cyprus problem through a bicommunal, bizonal federation and to articulate their concerns about security and implementation of the Plan with 'clarity and finality.'"

For roughly the next four years, to little avail, Cyprus muddled through a series of offers and counter-offers to restart serious negotiations even as the Greek Cypriots solidified their new status as a member of the EU, a status not extended to the Turkish Cypriots despite an EU pledge to try to help end the isolation of the north.

2008—New Hope

On February 24, 2008, 61-year-old Dimitris Christofias of the Progressive Party of Working People (AKEL) was elected to a five-year term as President of Cyprus. Mr. Christofias was educated in the Soviet Union and is a fluent Russian-speaker. He joined the communist-rooted AKEL party at the age of 14 and rose through its ranks to become leader in 1988. Christofias was elected president of the Cypriot House of Representatives in 2001 and won reelection in 2006.

Christofias's election had the backing of the Democratic (DIKO) Party, and the Socialist (EDEK) Party. Christofias, in part, tailored his campaign to opposing what he believed was an uncompromising approach toward the Turkish Cypriots by Papadopoulos and the stagnation in the attempt to reach a just settlement of the Cyprus problem. Although serious differences existed between the Greek Cypriot and Turkish Cypriot sides over a final settlement, Christofias took the outcome of the vote as a sign that Greek Cypriots wanted to try once again for an end to the division of the island. In his inaugural address, President Christofias expressed the hope of achieving a "just, viable, and functional solution" to the Cyprus problem. He said that he sought to restore the unity of the island as a federal, bizonal, bicommunal Republic, to exclude any rights of military intervention, to provide for the withdrawal of Turkish troops and, ultimately, the demilitarization of the island. Christofias also reaffirmed that the 2004 Annan Plan was null and void and could not be the basis for a future settlement.

After Christofias's election, Turkish Cypriot leader Mehmet Ali Talat, a long-time acquaintance of Christofias, said, "a solution in Cyprus is possible by the end of 2008."[3] He also declared that "the goal is to establish a new partnership state in Cyprus, based on the political equality of the two peoples and the equal status of two constituent states."[4] As early as 2004, Talat, as Turkish Cypriot prime minister, was credited for helping convince the Turkish Cypriots to support the Annan Plan and had been seen as perhaps the one Turkish Cypriot leader who could move the Greek Cypriots toward a more acceptable solution for both sides. For his efforts at the time, Talat, on April 17, 2005, was elected "president" of the TRNC over the UBP 's Dervis Eroglu, receiving 55.6% of the vote in a field of nine.

On March 21, 2008, Christofias and Talat met and agreed to establish working groups to address issues related to a comprehensive settlement, including governance and power-sharing, EU matters, security and guarantees, territory, property, and economic matters. They also created seven technical committees to address day-to-day issues of crime, economic and commercial matters, cultural heritage, crisis management, humanitarian matters, health, and environment. The two leaders also decided to meet in three months to review the work of the committees and groups and use their results to start direct negotiations under U.N. auspices. As a first confidence-building measure, they agreed to reopen the Ledra Street crossing between the northern and southern parts of Nicosia.

On July 2, 2008, the two leaders met and agreed in principle on a single national sovereignty and citizenship and decided to start full-fledged negotiations on September 3. On July 18, U.N. Secretary-General Ban Ki-moon named former Australian Foreign Minister Alexander Downer to be his Special Advisor on Cyprus and to lend the good offices of the U.N. to the negotiation process. On July 20, 2008, Turkish Prime Minister Recep Tayyip Erdogan, perhaps recognizing that Turkey's own future as a potential member of the EU was very much tied to a successful settlement on Cyprus, extended full support to Talat and said that "a comprehensive solution will be possible in a new partnership where the Turkish Cypriot people and the Turkish Republic of Northern Cyprus will equally be represented as one of the founder states. This new partnership will be built upon such indispensable principles as bizonality, political equality, and Turkey's effective guarantorship."[5] The last part of that statement sent red flags throughout Greek Cyprus and reignited the ongoing debate over the continued presence of some 30,000 Turkish military forces on the island and the intense desire on the part of the Greek Cypriots to have all Turkish troops removed. Nevertheless, on September 11, 2008, substantive negotiations on governance and power-sharing began.

2009—Storm Clouds

While the negotiations between Christofias and Talat appeared to get off to a fast start, the differences in positions quickly became apparent and the talks, although held on a regular basis, started to bog down. Talat wanted to pursue negotiations on the basis of the provisions of the old Annan Plan, while Christofias, mindful of the Greek Cypriot rejection of that plan, was keen to avoid references to it. Old differences quickly resurfaced. For instance, both sides differed over how a new united Cyprus would be created. The Greek Cypriots assumed the new unified state would evolve from the existing Republic of Cyprus. The Turkish Cypriots wanted the new state to be based on two equal "founding states." While the two sides seemed to agree on a 48-member Senate and a House proportionally based on population, they differed on how the executive would operate and what powers it would have. Greek Cypriots proposed the election of a president and vice president on the same ticket in a direct election for a six-year term. The president would be a Greek Cypriot for four years and the vice president would be a Turkish Cypriot; they would then rotate offices, with the Turkish Cypriot becoming president for two years. Turkish Cypriots proposed that the executive have two alternating presidents elected by the 48-member Senate. Turkish Cypriots were opposed to a single list of Greek Cypriot and Turkish Cypriot candidates to be elected by all of the people because then the Greek Cypriots, by virtue of their majority, would elect the Turkish Cypriot candidate.

Property issues also plagued the negotiations. Greek Cypriots who lost properties in the north insisted that the legal owner must have the right to decide how to deal with his property, while Turkish Cypriots believed that the current inhabitant must have priority and that the issue should be resolved through compensation, exchange, and restitution. The question of territory was also in dispute. The Turkish Cypriot side of the "green line" included approximately 37% of the island and included several areas, such as Varosha, Morphou, and Karpas, that had been almost 100% Greek Cypriot inhabited before the 1974 division. Greek Cypriots wanted that territory returned, which would have left the Turkish side controlling about 29% of the territory.

Next to the property issue, the issue of security guarantees continued to be one of the most difficult bridges to cross. The Greek Cypriots had long argued that all Turkish military forces would have to leave the island. They argued that the European Union (EU) could offer guarantees to all of its member states and even offer guarantees to third countries. Therefore, once north Cyprus was part of the EU, they saw no reason for guarantees from third countries (Turkey).[6] Turkish Cypriots and Turkey maintained that the 1960 Treaties of Guarantee and Alliance must be reaffirmed in any settlement and Turkish security guarantees should not be lifted until Turkey joined the EU because, without guarantees, the Turkish Cypriots would feel insecure due to their history with ethnic violence on the island in the 1960s.

As the negotiations dragged on well into 2009, it appeared that impatience, frustration, and uncertainty were beginning to mount against both Christofias in the south and Talat in the north. In March 2009, the Democratic Party (DIKO), one of the main coalition partners of President Christofias's AKEL, held party elections. Hard-line candidates won all three posts contested— deputy leader, vice president, and general secretary. After the elections, some wanted their party to withdraw from the coalition. The outcome of this vote left many wondering whether Christofias would face difficulties in gaining approval for any agreement he would reach with Talat. In the north, parliamentary elections were held on April 19, 2009. The opposition UBP won 26 out of the 50 seats in the parliament. Talat's Republican Turkish Party (CTP), in alliance with the United Forces (BG), placed second, with 15 seats. While some claimed that the outcome of the vote could be attributed to popular disenchantment with the slow pace of the settlement process, economic issues and the government's failure to end the international isolation of the north also played a significant role. The election also propelled UBP Party leader Dervis Eroglu into the forefront of the presidential elections scheduled for April 2010. Eroglu had already staked out what seemed to be a harder-line approach and said that he was not against negotiations with the Greek Cypriots, but that the process should be based on the "reality that there are two equal sovereign states," adding that "our people are not condemned to unite with the Greek Cypriot side. Our right to separate is just as valid as our right to unite."[7] Interestingly, it was reported that on April 21, Turkish Prime Minister Erdogan and other Turkish leaders, perhaps sensing a more difficult time ahead in the negotiations and the EU's concern that Turkey needed to play a more constructive role in helping the negotiations, said that it would be wrong for the new government (of northern Cyprus) to end the negotiations or to continue the negotiations on a basis different from the one that has been followed so far and that they would not support a move that would weaken the hand of Talat.[8]

Those two political events in the spring of 2009 seemed to have hamstrung the ability of either side to take the dramatic steps needed to boost the negotiations into a final phase. Mr. Talat, on the one hand, now had a less sympathetic parliament to deal with, one whose disapproval of any agreement would likely play an important role in any referenda in the north. Mr. Christofias, on the other hand, had one party of his governing coalition already shifting toward a more hard-line stance that could restrict his ability to offer the kind of concessions needed for a final deal, and another that was complaining that it was not being adequately consulted on the President's negotiating strategy.

For the remainder of 2009, Christofias and Talat continued to meet and, for some, gave the appearance that they both still held out hope, against mounting odds, that a settlement could be reached. There were at times some small signs of movement. Christofias seemed to become a little more flexible on the idea of a rotating presidency, and in September 2009, Talat seemed to have made a significant concession in agreeing to accept the Greek position for a president and vice president even though he continued to have doubts about direct popular voting, preferring that the president and vice president be elected by the Senate.

By the end of 2009, however, perspectives on both sides of the island seemed to have begun to change. Some suggested that the Greek Cypriots sensed that the talks could not produce a desired outcome before the April 2010 elections in the north and thus the negotiations were likely to have to begin anew, possibly with an entirely different Turkish Cypriot leadership. Under that scenario, many Greek Cypriots, including members within the political parties of the governing coalition, seemed leery of weakening their hand by offering further concessions. Although there were some who feared that Christofias, in an attempt to help his friend Talat secure reelection, would offer too much to the Turkish side, it was unclear whether Christofias was willing to risk his political standing for something even he had begun to feel was unattainable. Some Turkish Cypriots, on the other hand, appear to have begun to think that the Greek Cypriot side would not offer Talat a negotiated settlement, betting from the opinion polls in the north that Eroglu would win the April elections and would pull back from serious negotiations, at least for a while as he consolidated his new government and re-ordered his strategy. The Greek Cypriots could then blame the anticipated hard-liners in the north and their presumed patrons in Ankara if the talks collapsed.

2010—Declining Expectations

As Cyprus entered the new year, it appeared that the window of opportunity to reach a final settlement, at least between Christofias and Talat, was closing fast. Despite the fact that the two sides had been in negotiations for almost 18 months and in close to 60 meetings, they appeared to have very little to show for their efforts. In his new year message to the Greek Cypriots, Christofias suggested that while some progress had been made in a few areas, the two sides were not close to a settlement. Despite the initial gloom, he pledged to continue to hold intensified discussions with Talat.

In what appeared to be a curious move, on January 7, 2010, Turkish Cypriot leader Talat tabled a new proposal apparently intended to represent the Turkish Cypriot negotiating position in advance of the new round of talks. Reports indicated that although it appeared that Talat may have agreed to several additional Greek proposals, including cross-community voting, the Greek Cypriot side was apparently taken somewhat by surprise at Talat's remaining proposals because they appeared to differ from what had been on the negotiating table up to that point. For instance, the Talat proposal called for a 3:2 rotating presidency (three years for a Greek Cypriot president and two years for a Turkish Cypriot president) instead of the 4:2 proposal on the table. Similarly, the Turkish Cypriot proposal for a cabinet included a 7 (Greek Cypriot):5 (Turkish Cypriot) split instead of a 6:3 split. The proposal also called for basic freedoms for all Turkish settlers who had come to the island and two separate flight information regions (FIRs), or air traffic control centers, instead of one for the entire island. The press reported that while President Christofias shared the proposals with his coalition partners, he would not even discuss them in public, indicating to some that he was disappointed that the talks might actually be moving backward.

Although seen by some as intended to jolt the negotiations into high gear, there has been some other speculation as to why Mr. Talat would have offered a proposal that he knew would likely be deemed unacceptable to the Greek Cypriots. One theory was that Ankara felt its own best chance to keep their accession talks with the EU alive was to have Talat win reelection as president of Turkish Cyprus. To do that, Talat needed to look as if he were taking a more realistic and perhaps, for some, a harder-line position in advance of the elections in the north. Another theory was that while Talat himself was not wedded to the provisions of the proposal, he knew that if he offered them and they were rejected by the Greek Cypriots, he could argue that the harder-line negotiating position advocated by his opponent Dervis Eroglu would not only not produce a positive outcome for Turkish Cypriots, it could very well cause the collapse of the negotiations altogether.

Despite what appeared to be a setback for the negotiations, both Christofias and Talat agreed to schedule six negotiating sessions through the month of January, although the backlash against the Turkish Cypriot proposals began at the same time and Christofias admitted that there was no aim to solve the [Cyprus] problem before the April vote in the north. The lack of public discussion of the Talat proposals by Christofias, however, was not the case with others. A spokesperson for the DIKO Party said that the Turkish Cypriot proposals fell outside the defined framework and "effectively torpedoed the negotiations."[9] Others suggested that the proposals were written in Ankara and forced on Talat, which once again revealed the true position of Turkey in the negotiations.

The intensive dialogue between Christofias and Talat resumed on January 11, 2010, but after three sessions the talks seemed to be at a standstill. On January 20, Christofias sent a letter to the five permanent members of the United Nations Security Council and heads of the EU member states complaining about the new Turkish Cypriot negotiating positions. In his letter, Christofias stated that the Turkish Cypriot [proposals] "show that the Turkish Cypriot side supports positions which contravene the agreed basis and sensitive balances which have been shaped during decades of negotiations. It is not possible to expect the Greek Cypriot side to accept positions which are beyond the balances."[10] Interestingly, in his letter, President Christofias, in arguing against each of the provisions of the Talat proposal, argued how they differed not from a Greek Cypriot negotiating position, but from the 2004 Annan Plan, which Christofias had insisted could not necessarily be the basis for an agreed settlement. For some, and although Christofias referred to "sensitive balances" in addition to the Annan Plan, this raised the question of whether the Greek Cypriot position on, for instance, governance was in fact the Annan plan.

Shortly after the Christofias letter was sent to the Security Council, U.N. Secretary-General Ban Ki-moon, perhaps sensing that the talks were about to stall, announced that he would travel to the island. On February 2, 2010, Secretary-General Ban arrived in Cyprus amid cautious speculation as to the meaning of the visit. In his arrival statement, Ban said that he was there to provide "personal support" because it was "important to recognize how important it is to continue to build momentum on what the leaders have achieved up to now" and that both sides needed more "courage and determination in the period ahead."[11] In his comments at a luncheon for the Secretary-General, Talat stated, "time is working against the settlement ... external developments as well as growing disillusionment among Turkish and Greek Cypriots make the solution more complex and difficult to attain."[12]

Although the visit of the U.N. Secretary-General failed to produce any tangible results, the two Cypriot leaders kept the negotiation process going with an agreement to meet at least four or five times through March 2010. However, it was clear that the gap between their respective positions seemed to be insurmountable and domestic political troubles continued to mount for both. In the north, opinion polls continued to suggest that Talat might not win reelection. In the south, Christofias's coalition partner EDEK threatened to quit the government over the very fundamental issue of whether a new, united Cyprus should have a rotating presidency, an issue long on the table. On February 9, 2010, EDEK's central committee voted to leave the coalition, claiming that, in their opinion, "the President has been following a mistaken strategy which the other side is using to its own advantage."[13] EDEK argued that the concessions Christofias made regarding a rotating presidency and the acceptance of 50,000 settlers had to be withdrawn. Soon after the EDEK decision, some factions within the DIKO party, the other member of the governing coalition, began agitating for a similar vote to leave the government, citing very similar reasons, including their disagreement over a rotating presidency. On February 23, the DIKO central committee met but decided to remain in the coalition for the present.

At the same time that the coalition parties were wrestling with their own internal politics, on February 19, 2010, the Greek Cypriot House of Representatives adopted a decision that essentially rejected the Turkish Cypriot and Turkish position that the 1960 Treaties of Guarantee and Alliance should remain in any final settlement, once again reiterating that no Turkish military forces could remain on the island after a settlement and that Turkey would no longer have a right to intervene in Cyprus. This action prompted a counter-resolution in the Turkish Cypriot parliament on February 24 accusing the Greek Cypriots of acting in bad faith and taking an unacceptable approach.

Near the end of February and in early March, two interesting developments took place related to the Cyprus issue. Perhaps sensing that the negotiations were not progressing favorably and in reaction to the accusations by some Greek Cypriots that the proposals presented by Talat in January were driven by Ankara, Turkish Prime Minister Erdogan invited Greek Cypriot media representatives to Turkey to meet with him to discuss Turkish views on the Cyprus peace process. During the meeting, which was unprecedented, it was reported that Erdogan spoke about his support for a bizonal, bicommunal federation; the eventual withdrawal of Turkish troops from the island; and a pledge of Turkish support for a "lasting comprehensive settlement" at the earliest possible time. [14] Erdogan's comments were mostly seen as positive support for the continuation of the negotiations and read by some in Cyprus as an indication that even if Talat was not reelected in April, his successor would not be allowed to "walk out of the talks."[15]

On March 11, a second development with potentially significant impact occurred. After returning from meetings in Ankara, Turkish Cypriot "foreign minister" Tahsin Ertugruloglu broke with his UBP party and announced his intention to run for president. While some believe Ertugruloglu has little chance of winning, his candidacy could pose a threat to Eroglu's voting base and raises the question again of Ankara's preference to see Talat reelected, as few believe Ertugruloglu would have made the decision to enter the race without, if not the approval, at least the acquiescence of Ankara.

On March 30, the last formal negotiating session between Christofias and Talat until the elections in the north concluded with apparently no new developments. In the run-up to the final session there was some speculation that both sides would issue a joint statement assessing the negotiations up to that point and perhaps even announcing some of the areas in which agreement between Christofias and Talat had been achieved. Speculation was that Talat, trailing his election opponent by 15 points in a poll taken on March 30, had wanted something positive to take into the final days of his reelection campaign and had presented Christofias a report summarizing what the Turkish Cypriots understood to have been achieved. Christofias, however, was already under pressure from his coalition partner, DIKO, and former coalition partner, EDEK, not to issue such a statement. Leaders from the opposition DISY party said they were not supportive of issuing such a statement until it had been reviewed by the Greek Cypriot National Council at a meeting scheduled for April 7.

On March 30, Christofias and Talat issued a short statement suggesting that they had indeed made some progress in governance and power sharing, EU matters, and the economy, but they did not go beyond that. Although this may have been the last time both Chritofias and Talat would meet, they stated that they were confident that they could overcome their divergent options and "reach a comprehensive settlement."[16] In what appeared to be a final friendly jest to Talat, Christofias announced that he would like to see Talat at the negotiating table after April 18. Perhaps as a sign of just how difficult things will be for Chritofias down the road, his comment was immediately criticized by the leadership of EDEK as lending support to an illegal election in the north.

Assessment

As March 2010 began, little progress had been achieved or, at least, had been acknowledged by both sides. In a March 19, 2010, speech to the citizens of Cyprus, President Christofias admitted that "the negotiations had not yet produced the anticipated result ... and that while the convergences have been achieved in the governance chapter, fewer have been achieved in the economy and EU chapters and even less in property."[17] And, with only a few negotiating sessions remaining before the April 18 elections in the north, few observers expected much to happen between then and the agreed final formal negotiating session before the break for the elections, which was scheduled for March 30.

The election of President Christofias in 2008 ushered in a period of higher expectations for a settlement than at any time since 2004, when the Annan Plan was considered by both Cypriot communities. The personal relationship between Christofias and Talat and their personal commitments to finding a solution to the Cyprus problem suggested that if these two leaders could not achieve a negotiated settlement, not perfect for either side but acceptable to both, then it might take a long time before two like-minded leaders would again find themselves in a position to find a way to unify the people of Cyprus.

Yet, after 18 months and more than 60 meetings and despite the strong commitment, good intentions, and warm relations between the two leaders, progress in the talks seems to have fallen victim to the harsh realities of almost four decades of separation, mistrust, misunderstanding, and in some cases, indifference to the need for a final settlement and unification of the island. Even a possible change in leadership in the north, and thus perhaps a different negotiating strategy and more uncertainty for the future, did not appear to be enough of an incentive to overcome the differences to find a final solution.

The inability of these two pro-solution leaders to reach an acceptable accommodation has led some observers to question whether a settlement can actually be achieved at all. In fact, the International Crisis Group (IGC), in a report published in the fall of 2009, suggested that after all the fits and starts of the current round of negotiations, "the island may be accelerating a slide toward permanent partition and that some elements in both communities given 36 years of futility and the wide differences of opinion over each item on the table from property rights to Turkish settlers to governance, may be willing to concede the possibility of a permanently divided island."[18] Such a final outcome is one many observers feel would be a disaster for all sides on the island, as well as those with direct interest in a solution, such as the EU and Turkey. In his March 18 speech to the nation, Christofias referred to such talk and stated that abandoning the negotiations "would be a disastrous mistake ... and that he would not seek reelection to a second term as President if there was no solution to the Cyprus problem by 2013."[19]

Some say the lack of a final settlement would not necessarily affect the benefits enjoyed by the people of the Republic of Cyprus as a member of the European Union and thus there is less of an incentive to negotiate away parts of their authority and power to govern. Yet, without a settlement, it would seem that potential economic opportunities and growth across the entire island may not materialize. In addition, Greek Cypriots will be less likely to reclaim contested property in the north or at least receive fair compensation for it. A recent decision by the European Court of Human Rights (ECHR) to recognize the Immovable Property Commission (IPC) in the north means that all efforts to settle claims for compensation or restitution by Greek Cypriots who fled to the south as a result of events in 1974 and lost their property would have to be exhausted in the IPC before claims could be filed with the ECHR. This decision by the ECHR, however, could force many Greek Cypriots who had hoped to avoid dealing with Turkish Cypriots or Turkey in seeking compensation or restitution for their property, to now demand a political settlement that includes remedies for property claims. Finally, the failure to reach a settlement would mean that Greek Cypriots may forever face a large and powerful Turkish army just a few kilometers away from infamous "green line."

For their part, the lack of a settlement for Turkish Cypriots could likely mean further isolation, little or no recognition for the TRNC, no EU membership, and continued dependence on Turkey for financial assistance.

For some on both sides, these may be risks worth taking. As the ICG pointed out in its report, there appears to be a growing younger generation on both sides of the island who have never interacted with the other and see no reason to, do not have as much of a stake in the property issue, and may not wish to face the uncertainties and potential problems that a settlement neither side likes, but accepts, could create.

Outside of the island, no one involved in the Cyprus issue wants to see the negotiations end or take such a significant step backward that it would take years to return to where the negotiations currently stand, even if many are not sure just how much progress toward a solution has actually been achieved. These interested third parties certainly do not want both Cypriot sides to conclude that maybe a permanent separation is the least painful solution because such an outcome will likely affect not only Cypriot-to-Cypriot relations but also Cyprus-Turkey, Greece-Turkey, EUTurkey, and NATO-EU relations. Earlier in the month, Turkish Prime Minister Erdogan had suggested that, as a way to move the negotiations forward, a five-party international conference be held to try to help settle the major differences between the two Cypriot sides. The initial Greek Cypriot reaction was that such a conference was not needed and that a solution would have to come from the Cypriots themselves. However, in his March 18 speech, Christofias did seem to suggest that an international conference that included the permanent members of the

U.N. Security Council, the EU, Greece, Turkey, and the two Cypriot sides could focus on what he termed the international aspects of the problem, namely troop withdrawals, settlers, and future security guarantees.

Now that the formal negotiations have ended all interested parties will focus on the April 18 elections in the north and, depending on the outcome of those elections, will continue to express the desire for the talks to resume as soon as possible after that. But even after the outcome of the elections in the north determines who will be seated at the negotiating table and when the negotiations will resume, the difficult work of finding the elusive settlement will begin anew and will not likely be any easier.

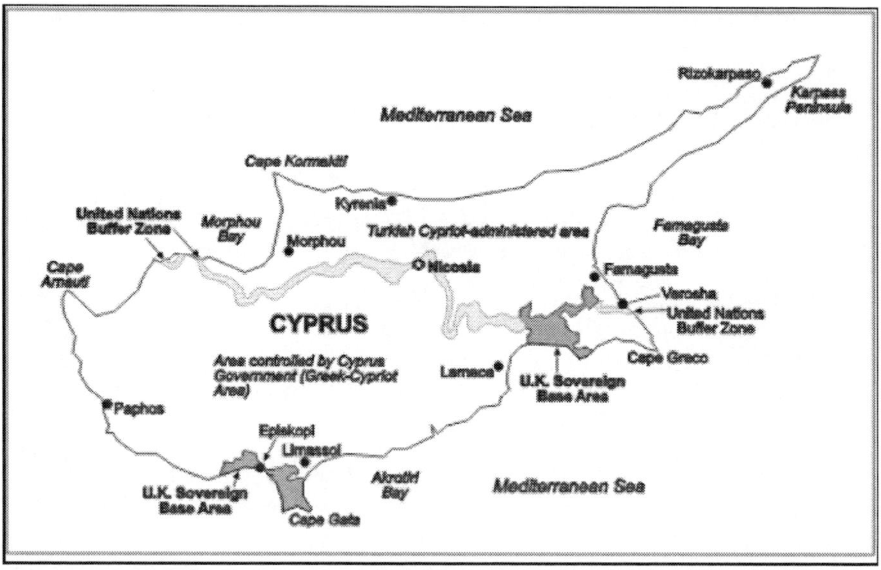

Source: Map Resources. Adapted by CRS.

Figure 1. Map of Cyprus

End Notes

[1] Parts of this chapter are drawn from a more comprehensive history of the Cyprus negotiations found in CRS Report RL33497, *Cyprus: Status of U.N. Negotiations and Related Issues*, by Carol Migdalovitz.

[2] Turkey officially refers to its action as a "peace operation." The Greek Cypriots and much of the international community refer to it as an "invasion." According to the International Institute for Strategic Studies, *The Military Balance—2009*, Turkey still has 36,000 troops on the island. However, the Greek Cypriots claim that the figure is 42,000 to 44,000.

"Defense Committee: UNFICYP Figures on Occupying Troops are False," Cyprus News Agency, February 6, 2009, BBC Monitoring European.

[3] "I am Hopeful about a Solution, TRNC President Talat," *Anatolia*, February 25, 2008, BBC Monitoring European, February 26, 2008.

[4] Letter to the Editor, *Financial Times*, March 5, 2008.

[5] "Erdogan Warns Against Attempts to Water Down Parameters of Cyprus Settlement," *Turkish Daily News*, July 21, 2008.

[6] "Cypriot FM: No Derogations from Acquis During a Solution," Cyprus News Agency, November 14, 2008, BBC Monitoring European, November 17, 2008.

[7] Jean Christou, "Eroglu Back on the Scene with Return to UBP Head," *Cyprus Mail*, December 2, 2008.

[8] Comments of Turkish President Gul and Prime Minister Erdogan as reported in *Radikal*, April 22, 2009 and cited in *Cyprus: Reunification or Partition,* International Crisis Group, September 30, 2009.

[9] "Backlash against Turkish side's proposals begins," *Cyprus Mail*, January 9, 2010.

[10] Letter of the Greek Cypriot President Christofias to the five permanent members of the U.N. Security Council and heads of EU member states, January 20, 2010.

[11] Remarks of United Nation secretary General Ban Ki-moon at a joint press conference at the Nicosia airport, February 2, 2010.

[12] Comments of Turkish Cypriot leader Mahmet Ali Talat at the luncheon for U.N. Secretary General Ban Ki-moon, February 2, 2010.

[13] "EDEK quits government," *Cyprus Mail*, February 9, 2010.

[14] Account of the press conference between representatives of Greek Cypriot media and Turkish Prime Minister Recep Tayyip Erdogan as reported in the *Cyprus Mail*, March 2, 2010.

[15] "What was the meaning behind Erdogan's words?," *Cyprus Mail*, March 7, 2010.

[16] "Leaders convinced they can reach a settlement," *Cyprus Mail*, March 31, 2010.

[17] Public address to the people of Cyprus by President Christofias, March 18, 2010.

[18] *Cyprus: Reunification or Partition?* Europe Report 201, The International Crisis Group, September 30, 2009.

[19] Op. Cit., speech by President Christofias.

In: Greece: Background, Debt, and Cyprus Issues ISBN: 978-1-61728-866-1
Editors: Brian D. Newmann

Chapter 4

CYPRUS: STATUS OF U.N. NEGOTIATIONS AND RELATED ISSUES*

Carol Migdalovitz

SUMMARY

Cyprus has been divided since 1974. Greek Cypriots, 76% of the population, live in the southern two-thirds of the island and lead the internationally recognized Republic of Cyprus. Turkish Cypriots, 19% of the populace, live in the "Turkish Republic of Northern Cyprus" (TRNC), recognized only by Turkey, with about 36,000 Turkish troops providing security. United Nations peacekeeping forces (UNFICYP) maintain a buffer zone between the two. Since the late 1970s, the U.N., with U.S. support, has promoted negotiations aimed at reuniting the island as a federal, bicommunal, bizonal republic. The U.N. Secretary-General's April 5, 1992, "Set of Ideas" was a major, but unsuccessful, framework for negotiations for a settlement. Next, both sides accepted U.N. confidence-building measures only in principle and they were not recorded or implemented.

The prospect of Cyprus's European Union (EU) accession and its eventual membership intensified and complicated settlement efforts. On November 11, 2002, Secretary-General Kofi Annan submitted a comprehensive settlement

* This is an edited, reformatted and augmented edition of a United States Congressional Research Service publication, Report RL33497, dated April 24, 2009.

Plan, but the two sides did not agree on it. After more negotiations, Annan announced on March 11, 2003 that his efforts had failed. Cyprus signed an accession treaty to join the EU on April 16.

The December 14, 2003, Turkish Cypriot parliamentary elections produced a new government determined to reach a settlement. After the U.N. led negotiations between the parties and with Greek and Turkish leaders present, Annan presented a final, revised Plan on March 31, 2004. In referenda on April 24, 76% of Greek Cypriot voters rejected the Plan, while 65% of Turkish Cypriot voters accepted it. Annan blamed President Tassos Papadopoulos, a Greek Cypriot, for the result. Cyprus joined the EU on May 1, 2004. More than two years later, Papadopoulos and Turkish Cypriot leader Mehmet Ali Talat agreed, on July 8, 2006, to discuss "issues that affect day-to-day life" and, concurrently, substantive issues. The accord was not implemented.

Dimitris Christofias's election as Cypriot president on February 24, 2008 ended the impasse. On March 21, he and Talat agreed to resume the settlement process, with working groups and technical committees. In September, they began direct negotiations for a solution to the Cyprus issue. Negotiations continue.

Some Members of Congress have urged the Administration to be more active, although they have not proposed an alternative to the U.N.-sponsored talks. After the 2004 referenda, the Administration worked to end the isolation of the Turkish Cypriots in order to diminish economic disparities between them and the Greek Cypriots and pave the way for reunification. Some Members questioned this policy. Members are maintaining their interest in Cyprus in the 111th Congress partly due to keen constituent concern.

Most Recent Developments

Settlement Talks

Cypriot President Dimitris Christofias and Turkish Cypriot leader Mehmet Ali Talat have been holding direct negotiations since September 2008, with either the U.N. Secretary-General's Special Advisor for Cyprus Alexander Downer or his deputy Taye-Brook Zerihoun present at the meetings. The two leaders' agenda includes the core issues of governance and power-sharing, property, the European Union, the economy, territorial security, and guarantees, and they are working their way through the issues to identify areas of convergence and divergence. Their aides, George Iacovou and Ozdil Nami, meet to write down the understandings reached and prepare for the leaders' sessions.

Christofias, a Greek Cypriot, complained that during negotiations on governance and power sharing Talat was trying to give more power to federal states and create a confederation instead of a federation.[1] Talat denies that he seeks a confederation. The two sides also differ on how a united Cyprus will be created. The Greek Cypriots insist that the Republic of Cyprus will evolve into a federal state, which will be its continuation, while the Turkish Cypriots say that united Cyprus will be a new state.

According to leaks of (Greek) Cypriot National Council documents particularly to right-wing media and some statements of officials, the two sides differ about the executive and its power. Greek Cypriots have proposed the election of a president and vice president on the same ticket in a direct election for a six-year term. The president will be a Greek Cypriot and the vice president will be a Turkish Cypriot; they will rotate offices, with the Greek Cypriot holding the presidency for four years and the Turkish Cypriot succeeding him for two years. A council of ministers will be jointly appointed by the president and vice president and be composed of six Greek Cypriots and three Turkish Cypriots. If the council cannot reach decisions unanimously, then a simple majority will rule, provided that it includes at least one Greek Cypriot and one Turkish Cypriot minister. A conflict resolution committee will include the president, vice president, and one minister from each community. The committee will try to reach solutions unanimously. Failing that, it will reach solutions by majority; failing that, the president will decide.[2]

Talat has said he has proposed that the executive have two alternating presidents elected by the Senate. He is opposed to a single list of Greek and Turkish candidates to be elected by all of the people because then the Greeks would elect the Turkish candidate.

With regard to the issue of property, which is critical for Greek Cypriots who lost properties in the north, Christofias insists that the legal owner must have the right to decide how to deal with his property, while Talat believes that the current inhabitant must have priority and that the issue should be resolved through compensation, exchange, and restitution.

On the issue of security guarantees, in November 2008, Cypriot Foreign Minister Markos Kyprianou explained that his government believes the European Union (EU) can offer guarantees to all of its member states and even offer guarantees to third countries. Therefore, he saw no reason for guarantees from third countries (Turkey).[3] Turkish Cypriots and Turkey maintain that the 1960 Treaties of Guarantee and Alliance must be reaffirmed in any settlement because, without guarantees, the Turkish Cypriots would feel insecure due to their history with ethnic violence on the island in the 1960s, and Turkish guarantees should not be lifted until Turkey joins the EU.

In general, the Greek Cypriots claim that Talat is not free to negotiate, but serves the will of Turkey, and Talat claims that Christofias is dependent on his anti-settlement coalition partners. Talat admits that the Turkish Cypriots' reliance on Turkey for external relations and economic survival makes him dependent on the mother state, but insists that Ankara is not issuing instructions to him.[4]

According to the Secretary-General's Special Advisor for Cyprus Alexander Downer, the two sides have agreed to confidence-building measures, including the crossing of ambulances in emergency cases, a committee on communications and liaison for criminal matters, an advisory board on the preservation of cultural heritage, and a U.N. Development Program project on water- saving.

Domestic Politics

After a two-hear hiatus, 70-year-old Dervis Eroglu made a political comeback in December 2008, when he was elected chairman of the opposition National Unity Party (UBP) in northern Cyprus. He previously had held the post for about 25 years and had served as "prime minister" of northern Cyprus seven times. Eroglu stated that he is not against negotiations with the Greek Cypriots, but that the process should be based on the "reality that there are two equal sovereign states." He added, "Our people are not condemned to unite with the Greek Cypriot side. Our right to separate is just as valid as our right to unite. We feel it is necessary to make alternative plans with the cooperation of Motherland Turkey." Eroglu charged that Talat had made a mistake when he accepted a single sovereignty and single citizenship for Cyprus.[5]

In parliamentary elections in the north on April 19, 2009, the UBP won an overwhelming victory of 26 out of 50 seats, Talat's Republican Turkish Party (CTP) in alliance with the United Forces (BG), placed second with 15 seats, the Democratic Party (DP) third with 5 seats, the Communal Democracy Party (TDP) fourth with two seats, and the Freedom and Reform Party (ORP), fifth with two seats. The result has been attributed to popular disenchantment with the slow pace of settlement process, to economic issues, and the government's failure to end the international isolation of the north. A new government is expected to be formed by mid-May.

Eroglu and said that he would continue to support negotiations, but wants to name someone to accompany the president at the talks. Talat retains authority to negotiate as long as he is president – until April 2010. However, the Turkish Cypriot parliament will have to vote to refer an agreement to a referendum and that may now be difficult.

Turkey will likely to exercise a restraining influence on Eroglu. On April 21, Turkish Prime Minister Recep Tayyip Erdogan said, "It would be wrong for the new government (of northern Cyprus) to end the negotiations or to continue the negotiations on a basis different from the one that has been followed so far.... The process must continue exactly as before.... We will never support a move that would weaken the hand of Talat." Turkish President Abdullah Gul also signaled his support for Talat.

Meanwhile, the Democratic Party (DIKO), the main governing partner of President Christofias's Progressive Party of Working People (AKEL), held party elections in March 2009. Hard-line candidates won all three posts contested – deputy leader, vice president, and general secretary; some want their party to withdraw from the coalition. The vote was interpreted as a defeat for party leader and Speaker of the House of Representatives Marios Garoyian, who has been relatively circumspect in his criticism of the President. Christofias may face difficulties in gaining approval for any agreement he may reach with Talat.

Other

In November 2008, several incidents occurred in an exclusive economic zone (EEZ) that Cyprus had declared with Egypt, off the south coast of the island. Turkish warships accosted Panamanian-flagged ships with Norwegian oceanographic researchers under contract to the Republic of Cyprus aboard who were conducting a survey for possible oil and gas reserves and forced the ships to cease operations and withdraw. Cyprus claimed that it was exercising its sovereign right to conduct surveys and that Turkey violated international law. Cyprus complained to the U.N. Turkey alleged that the research was being conducted inside its continental shelf and argued that the Greek Cypriots had no right to explore for oil or gas before reaching a settlement with the Turkish Cypriots on the status of the island.

In fall 2008, the Cypriot National Guard cancelled its annual Nikiforos exercises and the Turks cancelled their Toros military exercises on Cyprus. These acts conform with an established pattern: exercises occur when no progress is being made or no talks held and they are cancelled when talks are ongoing in order not to disturb a favorable climate.

U.S. Policy

On a visit to Turkey in March 7, Secretary of State Hillary Rodham Clinton said, "the United states continues to support the U.N.-sponsored talks now taking place to achieve a settlement of the Cyprus conflict based on reunification of the island as a bi-zonal, bi-communal federation." Her joint statement with Foreign Minister Ali Babacan also called for "ending the isolation of the Turkish Cypriots" in the context of supporting a settlement. (Greek) Cypriot officials then restated their view that "the so-called isolation of the Turkish Cypriots" is the result of the Turkish occupation.

President Barack Obama briefly encountered President Christofias on the sidelines of an European Union-U.S. summit in Prague on April 4. Then on April 6, President Obama addressed Turkish Grand National Assembly (parliament) in Ankara and said, "The United States is willing to offer all the help sought by the parties as they work towards a just and lasting settlement that reunifies Cyprus as a bizonal and bicommunal federation." Also in Prague, Secretary Clinton met Cypriot Foreign Minister Marcos Kyprianou. On April 15, she met Talat at the State Department. Talat said that he had asked the Secretary to support his call for a more active U.N. role, to appoint a special U.S. representative for Cyprus, and to contribute to efforts to lift the isolation of the Turkish Cypriot community. The State Department spokesman said that Clinton had "expressed her support for the efforts of both sides to build on the momentum and achieve a solution as soon as possible." He also said that it was not time to appoint a special coordinator for Cyprus. The Secretary met Kyprianou at the State Department on April 20. On the same day, Vice President Joe Biden met the foreign minister.

Some in Cyprus and Greece were dismayed by responses of Philip Gordon, nominee for Assistant Secretary of State for European and Eurasian Affairs, at his Senate Foreign Relations Committee confirmation hearing on

March 26. Gordon referred to a "Turkish presence in northern Cyprus" and noted that "there are a number of outside experts and the government of Cyprus who consider it an occupation." The Committee approved Gordon's appointment, but a Senate vote has been delayed due to a hold because of an issue unrelated to Cyprus.

BACKGROUND

The island Republic of Cyprus gained its independence from Great Britain in 1960. The 784,000 Cypriots are 77% of Greek ethnic origin, and 18% of Turkish ethnic origin. (Maronite Christians, Armenians, and others constitute the remainder.) At independence, the Republic's constitution defined elaborate power-sharing arrangements between the two main groups. It required a Greek Cypriot president and a Turkish Cypriot vice president, each elected by his own community. Simultaneously, a Treaty of Guarantee signed by Britain, Greece, and Turkey ensured the new Republic's territorial integrity and a Treaty of Alliance among the Republic, Greece, and Turkey provided for 950 Greek and 650 Turkish soldiers to help defend the island. However, at that time, the two major communities aspired to different futures for Cyprus: most Greek Cypriots favored union of the entire island with Greece (*enosis*), and Turkish Cypriots preferred to partition the island (*taksim*) and unite a Turkish zone with Turkey.

Cyprus's success as a new republic lasted from 1960-1963. After President (and Greek Orthodox Archbishop) Makarios III proposed constitutional modifications in favor of the majority Greek Cypriot community in 1963, relations between the two communities deteriorated, with Turkish Cypriots increasingly consolidating into enclaves in larger towns for safety. In 1964, Turkish Cypriots withdrew from most national institutions and began to administer their own affairs. Intercommunal violence occurred in 1963-64, and again in 1967. On both occasions, outside mediation and pressure, including that by the United States, appeared to prevent Turkey from intervening militarily on behalf of the Turkish Cypriots. On March 4, 1964, the U.N. authorized the establishment of the United Nations Peacekeeping Force in Cyprus (UNFICYP) to control the violence and act as a buffer between the two communities. It became operational on March 27 and still carries out its mission today. (See "U.N. Peacekeeping Forces" below for details.)

In 1974, the military junta in Athens supported a coup against President Makarios, replacing him with a more hardline supporter of *enosis*. In July, Turkey, citing the 1960 Treaty of Guarantee as a legal basis for its move, sent troops in two separate actions and, by August 25, took control of more than 36% of the island. This military intervention[6] had many ramifications. Foremost was the widespread dislocation of the Cypriot population and related refugee and property problems. The Athens junta fell, civilian government was restored in Athens and in Nicosia, Greece withdrew from NATO's military command to protest NATO's failure to prevent Turkey's action, and Turkey's civilian government entered an extended period of instability. U.S. relations with all parties, each of which blamed its fate on Washington's lack of support, suffered.

After 1974, Turkish Cypriots emphasized a solution that would keep the two communities separate in two sovereign states or two states in a loose confederation. In February 1975, they declared their government the "Turkish Federated State of Cyprus" (TFSC). In 1983, Turkish Cypriot leader Rauf Denktash declared the "Turkish Republic of Northern Cyprus" (TRNC)—a move considered by some to be a unilateral declaration of independence. Only Turkey has recognized the TRNC. Denktash argued that creation of an independent state is a necessary precondition for a federation with the Greek Cypriots. He ruled out a merger with Turkey and pledged cooperation with U.N. settlement efforts.

Settlement Efforts and Other Developments

After 1974, U.N. negotiations focused on reconciling the two sides' interests and reestablishing a central government. They foundered on definitions of goals and ways to implement a federal solution. Turkish Cypriots emphasized bizonality and the political equality of the two communities, preferring two nearly autonomous societies with limited contact. Greek Cypriots emphasized the freedoms of movement, property, and settlement throughout the island. The two parties also differed on the means of achieving a federation: Greek Cypriots wanted their internationally recognized national government to devolve power to the Turkish Cypriots, who would then join a Cypriot republic. For the Turkish Cypriots, two entities would join, for the first time, in a new federation. These views could affect resolution of property, citizenship of Turkish settlers, and other legal issues. Since 1974, there have been many unsuccessful rounds of U.N.- sponsored direct and indirect negotiations to achieve a settlement:

1977 Makarios-Denktash Meeting

Agreed that (1) Cyprus will be an independent, nonaligned, bicommunal, federal republic; (2) each administration's control over territory will be determined in light of economic viability, productivity, and property rights; (3) freedom of movement, settlement, and property will be discussed; and (4) powers and functions of the central federal government would safeguard the unity of the country.

1979 Kyprianou-Denktash Communique

Cypriot President Spyros Kyprianou (Makarios 's successor) and Rauf Denktash agreed to talk on the basis of the 1977 guidelines and address territorial and constitutional issues, giving priority to Varosha (Maras to Turkish Cypriots) and demilitarization, and to eschew union in whole or part with any other country. (Varosha is a formerly prosperous tourist area just north of the U.N. buffer zone. See map at end of report.)

1984 Proximity Talks

After the 1983 declaration of the "TRNC," U.N. representatives conducted proximity or indirect talks on constitutional arrangements, withdrawal of foreign troops, and the status of international treaties and guarantees.

1988-89 Talks

After futile informal direct talks, Cypriot President George Vassiliou and Denktash submitted papers that hardened positions. In April 1989, U.N. Secretary-General Javier Perez de Cuellar proposed separate meetings. Denktash balked, but the U.N. believed the parties had agreed to "separate and periodic joint meetings." In June, Perez de Cuellar circulated draft ideas for an agreement. Turkish Cypriots argued that the U.N. had exceeded its good offices role and would accept only a document drafted by the parties.

March 1990-April 1992

U.N. Security Council Resolution 649, May 13, 1990, reaffirmed the Secretary-General's right to make suggestions. It referred to the federal solution as bicommunal in its constitutional aspects and bizonal in its territorial aspects—the first U.N. reference to bizonality, a key concept for the Turkish Cypriots, who believe that it responds to their desire for separation.

In June 1991, Perez de Cuellar called for an international meeting. On August 2, President George H.W. Bush announced that Greece and Turkey had agreed to a U.N. conference on Cyprus. The Secretary-General insisted, however, that the two sides be within range of agreement first. The Greek and Turkish Prime Ministers were unable to find common ground and, on October 8, de Cuellar reported that a conference was not possible. He blamed the failure on Denktash's assertion that each side possessed sovereignty, which U.N. resolutions attribute solely to the Republic.

Set of Ideas

Secretary-General Boutros Boutros-Ghali's April 1992 Report to the Security Council presented a framework for a settlement, which he referred to as a "Set of Ideas." The Secretary-General suggested a bizonal federation of two politically equal communities, possessing one international personality and sovereignty. A bicameral legislature would have a 70:3 0 ratio of Greek Cypriots to Turkish Cypriots in the lower house and a 50:50 ratio in the upper house. A 7:3 ratio would prevail in the federal executive. Each community would be guaranteed to have a majority of the population and of land in its area. Non-Cypriot forces not foreseen in the 1960 Treaty of Alliance—that is, most Turkish troops—would withdraw. In June, Boutros-Ghali presented what diplomats referred to as a "non-map" of his territorial suggestions.

A revised U.N. draft provided for separate referenda in each community within 30 days of an agreement, an 18-month transitional period, withdrawal of Turkish troops, guarantees consistent with Conference on Security and Cooperation in Europe (CSCE) principles, an end of the Greek Cypriot trade

although de Soto did not think it was a good idea, Clerides and Denktash met on December 4 for the first time since August 1997. The two leaders agreed to begin direct talks with no preconditions, all issues on the table, and to continue until a comprehensive settlement is achieved. On December 5, Clerides attended a dinner at Denktash's residence, thereby becoming the first Cypriot president to travel to the north since 1974. Denktash reciprocated by visiting Clerides's home on December 29.

Developments, 2002-2003

On January 16, 2002, Clerides and Denktash agreed to hold intensive peace talks beginning January 21 at Nicosia Airport, a U.N. base. Annan's September 6 Report to the Security Council noted that "the elements of a comprehensive settlement ... exist," and "that the gaps dividing the parties can be bridged." Clerides observed, however, that there appeared to be no way of approaching sovereignty and whether there would be a new state or a continuation of the Republic of Cyprus. On September 16, Denktash proposed Belgium as a model for foreign affairs and Switzerland as a model for domestic affairs.

Annan Plan

The Secretary-General presented a draft of The Basis for Agreement on a Comprehensive Settlement of the Cyprus Problem, commonly referred to as the Annan Plan, on November 11, 2002. It called for a "new state of affairs," in which the "common state" government's relations with its two politically equal component states would be modeled on the Swiss federal example. It would have a single international legal personality. Component states would participate in foreign and EU relations as in Belgium. Parliament would have two 48-seat houses. Each state would have equal representation in the Senate. Seats in the Chamber of Deputies would be allocated in proportion to population, provided that no state would have less than 25% of the seats. A Presidential Council would have 6 members; the offices of President and Vice President would rotate every 10 months among its members. No more than two consecutive presidents could come from the same state. Greek and Turkish troops could not exceed a four-digit figure (9,999). U.N. peacekeepers would remain as long as the common state, with the concurrence of the component states, decides. Cyprus would be demilitarized. During a three-year transition, the leaders of the two sides would be co-presidents. The 1960 Treaties of Establishment, Guarantee, and Alliance would remain in force. There would be a single Cypriot citizenship and citizenship of a component state; residence in a component state could be limited by citizenship, but such limits would have restrictions. Provisions would be made for return or compensation of property. Turkish Cypriot territory would be reduced to 2 8.5% of the island.

Clerides and Denktash submitted comments. Greek Cypriot concerns included power-sharing, the length of the transition period, insufficient Greek Cypriot repatriation, and the large Turkish settler population. Turkish Cypriots criticized sovereignty provisions, the loss of water resources and territory, which would displace many Turkish Cypriots, and the return of Greek Cypriots to the north. Annan's December 10 revised Plan reduced the number of foreign troops and settlers and increased the number of returning Greek Cypriots, but reduced their numbers moving into Turkish Cypriot territory. He asked both sides to be in Copenhagen during an EU summit. Clerides and his National Council of all Greek Cypriot political party leaders were there, but Denktash went to Ankara for medical care and sent his "foreign minister" in his place. Annan had wanted a Founding Agreement signed by December 12, but this did not take place.

Turkish Cypriots demonstrated for EU membership for a reunified island, a settlement based on the U.N. Plan, and Denktash's resignation between November 2002 and February 2003. On January 2, 2003, Recep Tayyip Erdogan, Chairman of the Justice and Development Party that had won the November 2002 parliamentary elections in Turkey, called for heeding the wishes of the people and pointedly said that he did not favor the policy of "the past 30 to 40 years...."[8] Denktash and Clerides held talks from January 15 until mid-February 2003.

On February 21, Greece and Turkey began talks on security issues related to Cyprus. Annan presented his third revised plan on February 26. It included a British offer to transfer 45 square miles or almost half of its sovereign base areas on the island: 90% to the Greek Cypriots and 10% to the Turkish Cypriots, if the two sides agreed to the Annan Plan. Revisions allowed Turkish Cypriots to retain the Karpass Peninsula, with Greek Cypriots settling there as well. Turkish Cypriot territory would decrease to 28.2%, and the number of Greek Cypriots returning north would increase to 92,000, but be capped at 21% of that region's population at the end of 15 years, and the number of

Turkish settlers allowed to remain on the island would increase. Annan asked Denktash and the newly elected President of Cyprus Tassos Papadopoulos to permit separate, simultaneous referenda on the Plan on March 30.

On March 10, 2003, Annan met Papadopoulos and Denktash in The Hague. The next day, Annan announced that he had been unsuccessful. Papadopoulos wished to be sure that gaps in federal legislation and constituent state constitutions would be filled, that Greece and Turkey would commit to security provisions, and that there was time for a campaign on the referendum. He was prepared not to reopen substantive provisions if Denktash did the same. (On November 20, 2003, Papadopoulos asserted that he would not have signed even if Denktash had done so.[9]) Denktash objected to basic points of the Plan, would not put it to a referendum, and argued that negotiations should begin anew. Annan suggested that negotiations continue until March 28 and that referenda be held on April 6. The parties did not agree. Annan announced that it was not possible to achieve a settlement before Cyprus signed the EU accession treaty on April 16. Annan's April 1 Report said that Denktash "bears prime responsibility" for the failure, a conclusion echoed by U.N. Security Council Resolution 1575, April 14, 2003. On April 18, Annan stated the Plan could be amended, but it "must be accepted as a basis for negotiating first."

On April 23, the Turkish Cypriot administration opened border checkpoints. The Cypriot government declared the decision illegal, but facilitated free movement. Residents have since made millions of border crossings with very few incidents.

Papadopoulos said that he was ready to negotiate based on the Annan Plan if it were improved to take into account the Treaty of Accession to the EU and to create a more viable and workable solution. Denktash stated "there is nothing to discuss." In his November 12 Report, Annan reiterated that "no purpose would be served" in renewing his mission of good offices unless both Cypriot parties, Greece, and Turkey were ready to finalize negotiations on the basis of his February 2003 Plan and to put the results to referenda shortly thereafter.

2004 Referenda and After

On January 12, 2004, after meeting with Turkish officials, Denktash admitted, "The Annan Plan is still on the table...." On January 23, the Turkish National Security Council—the country's highest ranking military and civilian leaders—reiterated its determination to reach a solution with the Plan as a reference. [10] On January 24, Prime Minister Erdogan told Annan that Turkey wanted talks to resume to reach an agreement and hold referenda before May 1 (when Cyprus was scheduled to join the EU). Erdogan declared that if the two sides could not fill in all the "blanks," then Turkey would allow Annan to do so if the Greek Cypriots accept that as well.[11]

Following talks with Annan in New York, Papadopoulos and Denktash agreed to resume negotiations on February 19 on Cyprus. They failed to agree on revising the Plan in talks held until March 22. On March 17, Denktash said that he would not attend follow-on talks in Switzerland beginning on March 24, and later declared that he would campaign against an accord. "Prime Minister" Mehmet Ali Talat represented northern Cyprus. On March 29, Annan presented a final revised Plan. Changes called for a Presidential Council with six voting members and additional non-voting members to be decided by Parliament to exercise executive power. The offices of President and Vice President would rotate every 20 months. Greek Cypriots displaced in 1974 who return north would be limited to 18% of the population there; Turkish military forces on the island would be reduced to 6,000 over 42 months and further in subsequent years; when Turkey joins the EU, the number falls to 650 Turkish troops and 950 Greek troops. Greek Cypriots would have more property returned. Annan announced on March 31 that the Plan would be put to referenda on April 24.[12]

In an emotional speech on April 7, Papadopoulos rejected the Plan for a number of reasons. Among them were doubt about whether the Turkish parliament would ratify the settlement plan; belief that Turkish Cypriots would gain immediate benefits (i.e., the end of the Republic of Cyprus and creation of a United Republic of Cyprus), while the Greek Cypriots would only see gains in the future; restrictions on Greek Cypriot acquisition of property in northern Cyprus and on return of refugees there, and the denial of political rights of (Greek Cypriot) returnees to the north; Greek Cypriot insecurity due to the authorization of even a small number of Turkish troops and increased Turkish guarantor rights; doubt about the economic viability of the Plan and concern about its harm to the Greek Cypriot standard of living; and belief that the island would not really reunify because there would be two states living separately and governmental decision- making procedures could create "paralyzing impasses." Finally, Papadopoulos admitted his preference for a solution after Cyprus's accession to the EU when it would have more leverage over Turkey given Turkey's aspirations to become an EU member. [13]

The U.N., EU, and United States criticized Papadopoulos's speech as part of a distortion of and propaganda campaign against the Plan to feed the Greek Cypriots' sense of insecurity, and the three objected to government restrictions on broadcasting views favoring the Plan.[14] Greek Prime Minister Karamanlis half-heartedly endorsed the Plan, saying that positive elements outweighed "difficulties." As noted above, Denktash rejected the Plan, but "Prime Minister" Talat called for a "yes" vote. The Turkish government supported the Plan.

The United States and Britain tried to address the guarantee or insecurity issue with a U.N. Security Council resolution to replace UNFICYP with a U.N. Settlement Implementation Mission in Cyprus (UNSIMIC), and other measures. On April 21, Russia vetoed the draft, saying that, while it supported Annan's efforts, the Council should not act before the referenda and that the draft should have been discussed more. (Greek) Cypriot Foreign Minister George Iakovou had previously visited Russia to explain his government's opposition to the Annan Plan.

In referenda held on April 24, 76% of Greek Cypriot voters rejected the Plan, while 65% of Turkish Cypriot voters accepted it. Afterwards, Talat urged the international community to end northern Cyprus's isolation by lifting restrictions on trade, travel, sports, and flights in order for it to develop economically and attract foreign investment. He said that he would not seek international recognition of the TRNC because Turkish Cypriots voted for and want reunification of the island. (Greek) Cypriot officials argued that direct flights and exports from the north would not contribute to reunification and that it was the sovereign right of the Republic of Cyprus to determine legal ports of entry for persons, capital, and goods.

In his May 28, 2004 Report, Annan described developments leading to the referenda. He said that the Greek Cypriots' vote must be respected, but they need to demonstrate willingness to resolve the Cyprus problem through a bicommunal, bizonal federation and to articulate their concerns about security and implementation of the Plan with "clarity and finality." As a contribution to reunification, he called for the elimination of restrictions that have the effect of isolating the Turkish Cypriots. He concluded, "A solution ... also needs bold and determined political leadership on both sides of the island, as well as in Greece and Turkey, all in place at the same time, ready to negotiate with determination and to convince their people of the need to compromise." He criticized Papadopoulos in particular. On June 7, Papadopoulos wrote to Annan about "inaccuracies" in his Report, which Annan stood by.[15] The

Security Council has not endorsed the Report due to Russian objections on behalf of the Greek Cypriots.

In his September 24 Report, Annan stated that he still saw no basis for resuming his good offices mission, and that Greek Cypriot and Turkish Cypriot leaders had ceased contacts and signs of mutual distrust had reappeared. Annan asserted that he did not intend to appoint a new Special Advisor on Cyprus (to replace de Soto, who was reassigned).[16] On February 10, 2005, Annan observed that the Turkish side, particularly Erdogan, had indicated a possible readiness to resume talks. Annan urged Papadopoulos to put on paper the changes that he would want to have in the Plan. On March 21, 2005, Papadopoulos asserted,

> When the Greek Cypriot side gives in writing and in detail the changes it wants to a U.N. settlement plan, then the U.N. Secretary-General will decide if ... 'we are proving our political will for a settlement.' This means that he will have the right alone ... to ... decide if what we are asking for is reasonable, if it provides the basis for the resumption of his initiative.... We will not accept another mediating role of the U.N. Secretary-General. The national issues ... can(not) be ... solved through the mediation of a foreigner....[17]

He added that Cypriots must have a reasonable expectation of success in the next talks, which have to be well prepared.

On May 27, Annan again reported little sign of improvement. He maintained that Greek Cypriot litigation against those buying Greek Cypriot property in the north in southern courts and in the European Court of Human Rights against Turkey "poses a serious threat to people-to-people relationships and to the reconciliation process." Implicitly challenging a Greek Cypriot view, Annan asserted that the rotation of Turkish troops and equipment did not imply a "reinforcement" because numbers and types remain unchanged. Under Secretary-General for Political Affairs Kieran Prendergast visited Cyprus, Greece, and Turkey and reported on June 22 that there was neither a level of mutual confidence nor a disposition to compromise and that "launching an intensive new process prematurely would be inadvisable." Papadopoulos reportedly told Prendergast that he wanted to reopen most of the issues in the Annan Plan. On October 26, Papadopoulos said that he wanted a U.N. initiative with more active EU involvement. On November 1, Talat responded that the EU cannot promote a solution because it is not an "unbiased organization" since only the Greek Cypriot side is in the EU. In his November

technical committees and their agendas. The two leaders also decided to meet in three months to review the work of the committees and groups and use their results to start negotiations under U.N. auspices. In addition, they agreed to reopen the Ledra Street crossing between the northern and southern parts of Nicosia. Iakovou and Nami later decided to set up six working groups on issues related to a comprehensive settlement, including governance and power-sharing, EU matters, security and guarantees, territory, property, and economic matters, as well as seven technical committees to address day-to-day issues of crime, economic and commercial matters, cultural heritage, crisis management, humanitarian matters, health, and environment. On April 3, the Ledra Street crossing reopened for the first time since December 1963.

On April 11, the Secretary-General named Taye-Brook Zerihoun of Ethiopia as his Special Representative to Cyprus, head of UNFICYP., and Deputy Special Adviser.

On May 23, Christofias and Talat met in Zerihoun's presence to review progress in talks between bicommunal teams of experts (which began work on April 21). In their joint statement, the two leaders reaffirmed their commitment to a bizonal, bicommunal federation with political equality. The partnership will have a federal government with a single international personality as well as Greek- and Turkish-Cypriot constituent states of equal status. On July 2, they met and agreed ins principle on a single national sovereignty and citizenship.

On July 25, Christofias and Talat decided to start full-fledged negotiations on September 3. The solution reached would be subject to referenda in the two sides simultaneously. The two leaders also approved confidence-building measures in the areas of the environment, cultural heritage, crisis management, and criminal matters and gave instructions for their full and immediate implementation. In addition, they instructed their representatives to take up the issue of Limnitis/Yesilirmak and other crossings. After ceremonial talks on September 3, substantive negotiations on governance and power-sharing began on September 11.

On July 18, U.N. Secretary-General Ban Ki-moon named former Australian Foreign Minister Alexander Downer to be his Special Advisor on Cyprus.

OTHER FACTORS AFFECTING THE TALKS

Domestic Politics in Cyprus

Greek Cypriots

On February 16, 2003, Tassos Papadopoulos was elected President of Cyprus as the candidate of several parties: his right-wing Democratic Party (DIKO), the Progressive Party of Working People (AKEL/communist), the United Democratic Union of Cyprus (EDEK/Socialist), and the Greens. AKEL leader Dimitris Christofias, as President (Speaker) of the House, acted for the president when he was absent or incapacitated. The 1960 Constitution reserves the vice presidency for a Turkish Cypriot.

In the May 21, 2006, elections for the 56-seat unicameral (Greek) Cypriot House of Representatives, AKEL placed first with 31.16% of the vote and 18 seats (down two from 2001), and the opposition Democratic Rally (DISY) led by Nikos Anastasiadis was second with 30.33% and 18 seats (down one). Papadopoulos's DIKO was third, scoring gains with 17.91% of the vote and 11 seats (up 2). EDEK took 8.9 1% and 5 seats (up 1); the European Party (EVROKO), 5.73% and 3 seats (up 1); and the Greens, 1.95% and 1 seat. DIKO's gains as well as those of EDEK, EVROKO, and the Greens, which share Papadopoulos's views on a settlement, were seen as an endorsement of his hardline policies. Christofias was reelected Speaker.

The three-party (DIKO/AKEL/EDEK) coalition dissolved after AKEL decided on July 8, 2007 to nominate Christofias as a candidate for president in the February 2008 election because it disagreed with the government's handling of the Cyprus (settlement) issue. Four AKEL ministers resigned from the cabinet on July 11; their nonpartisan replacements included former Ambassador to the United States Erato Kozakou-Markoullis as Cyprus's first woman Foreign Minister.

On February 24, 2008, Soviet-educated, 61-year-old, Dimitris Christofias was elected to a five- year term as President of Cyprus in a second round of voting with 53.36% of the vote and the backing of his AKEL, DIKO, EDEK, and the United Democrats. Former Foreign Minister Ioannis Cassoulides of DISY placed second with 46.64% of the vote. Ousted President Papadopoulos and several other candidates had been eliminated in the first round of voting on February 17. Both Christofias and Cassoulides campaigned by opposing Papadopoulos's uncompromising policies of toward the Turkish Cypriots and stagnation in settlement efforts.

Christofias appointed ministers from AKEL, DIKO, and EDEK, reviving Papadopoulos's coalition. He named Markos Kyprianou of DIKO, a former European Commissioner of Health and Consumer Protection and Member of the European Parliament, and son of former President Spyros Kyprianou, to be foreign minister. DIKO party leader Marios Garoyian was elected Speaker of the House.

Turkish Cypriots

Rauf Denktash led northern Cyprus from 1975 to 2005. The December 14, 2003, parliamentary elections had produced a tie between supporters and opponents of the Annan Plan in the 50-seat legislature. A coalition of the Republican Turkish Party (CTP) and the Peace and Democracy Movement (BDH) had hoped to oust Denktash as negotiator and achieve a solution based on the Annan Plan by May 2004, when Cyprus was to enter the EU. Instead, a close race produced a coalition government with Mehmet Ali Talat as Prime Minister and Serdar Denktash, Rauf's son and head of the Democrat Party (DP), as Deputy Prime Minister and Foreign Minister. After several members resigned, the government was reduced to a minority and could not legislate. Early parliamentary elections were held on February 20, 2005. With an 80% voter turnout, the CTP took 44.45% of the vote and 24 seats, while the National Unity Party (UBP) won 3 1.71% and 19 seats, DP won 13.49% and 6 seats, and BDH 5.81% and 1 seat. Talat and Denktash formed a new coalition.

On April 17, 2005, Talat had been elected "President" of the TRNC with 55.6% of the vote to 22.7% for UBP'S Dervis Eroglu, in a field of nine. Ferdi Sabit Soyer of the CTP became Prime Minister.

On June 25, 2006, mid-term elections for vacancies changed the distribution of seats in parliament to CTP 25, UBP 17, DP 7, and BDH still 1. On September 8, three UBP deputies and one DP deputy resigned from their parties; CTP then ended its coalition with DP. The UBP and DP defectors formed the Freedom and Reform Party (ORP) or Free Party for short, chaired by Turgay Avgi. UBP and DP charged that unethical methods had been used to effect the change, and some suggested that the Justice and Development Party (AKP) ruling party in Turkey had assisted in the defections.[26] Soyer formed a new coalition of CTP and the Free Party; Avgi is Foreign Minister. UBP and DP then boycotted the parliament and, in January 2008, Serdar Denktash and the remaining DP deputies resigned from parliament.

Policies of Greece and Turkey

The "motherlands," Greece and Turkey, defend and protect their ethnic kin, and their bilateral relations, strained over Aegean Sea issues, have been further harmed because of Cyprus. On November 16, 1993, Greek Prime Minister Andreas Papandreou and (Greek) Cypriot President Clerides agreed to a still-effective joint defense doctrine whereby their governments would decide on the Cyprus issue jointly, Greece would include Cyprus in its defense plan, and any Turkish advance would lead to war between Greece and Turkey. Clerides announced in April 1994 that Greece would provide air cover for Cyprus, while Cypriot bases would refuel Greek Air Force planes, a naval base would be set up, and elite Greek troops would bolster land forces.

In July 1999, Greece and Turkey began a dialogue, excluding Cyprus and the Aegean, that has led to many bilateral accords and a rapprochement. In 2004, new Greek Prime Minister Costas Karamanlis said that a resolution of the Cyprus issue should not be a precondition for Turkey joining the EU or for improving Greek-Turkish relations. Some analysts have suggested that Athens has advised Nicosia that its actions must not harm Greece's national interest, defined as diminishing the Turkish threat to Greece by keeping Turkey on the path to EU membership. Therefore, in this view, Athens will tolerate any action by Nicosia in the EU short of the exercise of its veto power against Turkey's EU progress.

Meanwhile, Turkish governments had argued for years that the Cyprus problem was not acute because Turkish Cypriot security had been ensured since 1974, and that dialogue was the appropriate channel for resolution. Turks agree that their armed forces should not withdraw from Cyprus until Turkish Cypriots' rights are guaranteed effectively. In a policy shift in 2004, the Turkish government decided that no solution is not a solution and sought U.N. action. Turkey has promised $1.8 billion in aid to the TRNC over three years, from 2007 to 2009. In 2007, it provided approximately $571 million.

Some powerful circles in Ankara may create difficulties for Turkish Cypriot leader Talat's efforts to achieve a settlement. Then Chief of the Turkish General Staff General Yasar Buyukanit visited Cyprus on March 29, 2008, and stated, "Our soldiers are here for the security of the Turkish Cypriots and they will continue to be here. Reaching an agreement is not enough alone for withdrawal of (Turkish) soldiers from Cyprus.... We should see how safe Turkish Cypriots are. We should believe they are safe."[27] On April 11, Turkish Land Forces Commander General Ilker Basbug (now Chief of Staff) visited northern Cyprus and asserted that Cyprus is an issue concerning the security of Turkey and the Turkish Republic of Northern Cyprus; therefore, the 1960 Treaties of Guarantee and Alliance should not be diluted.

On July 20, 2008, Turkish Prime Minister Recep Tayyip Erdogan extended full support to Talat and said that "a comprehensive solution will be possible in a new partnership where the Turkish Cypriot people and the Turkish Republic of Northern Cyprus will equally be represented as one of the founder states. This new partnership will be built upon such indispensable principles as bizonality, political equality, and Turkey's effective guarantorship."[28] Greek Cypriots do not accept that the TRNC will be a "founder state" or Turkey's guarantorship and see the state as a continuation of the Republic of Cyprus. Cypriot President Christofias requested Secretary General Ban Ki-moon to appeal to Turkey "irrespective of my friend Mehmet Ali Talat's reaction, the key lies with Ankara. This way the Turkish Cypriot side will become more logical on the issues we are discussing on governance...."[29]

European Union[30]

A customs agreement between Cyprus and the European Community (EC) came into force in 1988. On July 4, 1990, Cyprus applied for EC membership. Turkish Cypriots objected because, by accepting the application, the EC recognized the Republic's government and not their own. Greece's EC membership and Turkey's lack thereof led Turks and Turkish Cypriots to view increased EC/EU involvement with Cyprus as favoring Greek Cypriots to their detriment.

The EU was to set a date for Cyprus's accession negotiations in January 1995. The EU preferred a prior settlement of the Cyprus issue, but was willing to begin talks without one. In December 1994, Greece had vetoed an EU-Turkey customs union and some Europeans demanded that the veto be lifted before addressing Cyprus's application for membership in the EU. On March 6, 1995, the EU separately ratified the customs union accord and scheduled accession talks with Cyprus. At Greece's insistence, the Greek Cypriot government of the Republic was the EU's interlocutor. Turkish Cypriots were excluded from accession talks.

On July 10, 1997, the European Commission reconfirmed that membership talks with Cyprus would open in 1998. On July 20, 1997, then

Turkish Deputy Prime Minister Bulent Ecevit and Turkish Cypriot leader Rauf Denktash issued a joint declaration, noting the July 10 statement and calling for a process of partial integration between Turkey and TRNC to parallel that of Cyprus and the EU.

On several occasions, then Greek Deputy Foreign Minister George Papandreou said that Greece would block the EU's eastward expansion (to Poland and the Baltic countries) if Cyprus were not accepted because it is divided. On November 10, 1998, the EU began accession negotiations with Cyprus. On July 10, 1999, Greek Alternate Foreign Minister Yiannos Kranidiotis said that Greece would not object to Turkey's EU membership candidacy if assured that Cyprus's accession would go ahead even without a solution. The EU Helsinki summit's conclusions on December 10, 1999, said, "If no settlement has been achieved by the completion of accession negotiations, the ... decision on accession will be made without the above (i.e., a settlement) being a precondition. In this the Council will take account of all relevant factors." The summit also affirmed Turkey's EU candidacy.

In December 2002, the EU concluded accession talks with Cyprus. At the same time, the EU and NATO agreed on EU use of NATO assets, stipulating that Cyprus would not take part in EU military operations conducted using NATO assets once it became an EU member because it is not a member of NATO nor of NATO's Partnership for Peace.[31] This agreement is referred to as Berlin Plus. After Cyprus became an EU member in 2004, however, the EU said that it could not restrict Cyprus's participation in EU operations cooperating with NATO. This led Turkey to veto Cyprus's participation in the EU's discussions with NATO on issues such as terrorism and its participation in an EU police mission in Kosovo, although it did not oppose EU-NATO cooperation there. Turkey's stance also has affected NATO-EU cooperation in Afghanistan.

Cyprus signed the Treaty of Accession to the EU on April 16, 2003, to become an EU member on May 1, 2004. An attached Protocol suspends the application of the *acquis communautaire* (EU rules and legislation) to those areas "in which the government of the Republic of Cyprus does not exercise effective control." On July 14, 2003, the (Greek) Cypriot parliament ratified the Treaty on behalf of the entire island.

On June 3, the European Commission had proposed measures to bring northern Cyprus closer to the EU, including €12 million (US$ 14 million) in aid. It suggested that the Turkish Cypriot Chamber of Commerce certify the movement of goods between Cyprus and the EU (to circumvent a de facto EU embargo on Turkish Cypriot goods that began with a 1994 European Court ruling that certificates of origin and sanitary quality issued by Turkish Cypriot authorities were not valid, in other words requiring Greek Cypriot certificates). The (Greek) Cypriot government authorized the Chamber only to issue certificates of origin, but said that exports required further certification to be done at legal (southern) ports to ensure that EU specifications were met. Denktash accepted the aid, but rejected the trade measures.

On November 5, 2003, the Commission's annual report on Turkey's progress toward accession warned that "absence of a settlement on Cyprus could become a serious obstacle to Turkey's EU aspirations," while the December 12 European Council (summit) declaration said that "a settlement would greatly facilitate Turkey's membership aspirations."

The EU regretted the Greek Cypriots' rejection of the Annan Plan and congratulated the Turkish Cypriots for their "yes" vote in the April 24, 2004, referenda. EU foreign ministers said that they were "determined to put an end to the isolation of the Turkish Cypriot community and facilitate the reunification of Cyprus by encouraging the economic development of the Turkish Cypriot community." They called on the Commission to submit proposals. "Green Line Regulations," adopted on April 29 and effective on August 23, require Greek Cypriot authorities to end restrictions on EU citizens' travel between the two parts of the island and allow Turkish Cypriots to export more products through the south. On May 1, Cyprus officially joined the EU. EU laws and regulations are suspended in the north.

On July 7, 2004, the Commission proposed additional measures to end the Turkish Cypriots' isolation and to help eliminate the economic disparities between the two communities on the island, including €259 million (US$307 million) in aid for 2004-2006 and preferences to allow direct trade between northern Cyprus and EU countries. The (Greek) Cypriot government agreed to the aid but rejected the trade measure as illegally based on an EU provision providing preferential treatment for third parties which, it argued, would allow the TRNC to acquire characteristics of state short of international recognition. The Greek Cypriots also insisted that all trade between the north and Europe be conducted via the south. The Turkish Cypriots viewed the EU aid and trade proposals as indivisible, arguing that aid without trade would not grow their economy and that required use of southern ports would force the north's economy southward and make it smaller over time.

In June 2005, the EU held unsuccessful talks to break the stalemate. The Greek Cypriots proposed that Varosha be returned to them with joint operation of the port at Famagusta and a moratorium on the sale of or construction on Greek Cypriot property in the north. They argued that opening northern ports and airports would lead to the development of separate economies and the permanent division of Cyprus. The Turkish Cypriots offered Varosha in return for open ports and airports in the north. In December, a draft European Commission declaration echoed the Greek Cypriot proposal and was opposed by the Turkish Cypriots.

On December 17, 2004, the EU had decided to begin accession talks with Turkey on October 3, 2005, welcoming its "decision to sign the Protocol regarding the adaptation of the Ankara Agreement (customs union), taking into account the accession of ten new Member States" (including Cyprus) "prior to the actual start of accession negotiations." On July 30, 2005, Turkey signed the Protocol but simultaneously issued a unilateral declaration, noting that its signature did not amount to recognition of the Republic of Cyprus or prejudice Turkey's rights and obligations emanating from the treaties of 1960.

On September 21, the EU declared that Turkey's unilateral declaration had no legal effect on its obligations under the Protocol; called for its full, non-discriminatory implementation, and the removal of all obstacles to the free movement of goods (meaning that Turkey must open its ports and airports to Greek Cypriot ships and planes); stated that the EU will evaluate implementation in 2006 and that failure to implement in full will affect progress of Turkey's accession negotiations with the EU; and noted that recognition of all member states is a component of the accession process and underlined the importance of normalization of relations between Turkey and all EU member states. Cypriot President Papadopoulos expressed satisfaction with the EU declaration's non-linkage of Turkey's recognition of Cyprus to a solution to the Cyprus problem.

Turkish Cypriot leader Talat was disappointed that the declaration did not call on the Republic to lift restrictions on the north. The Turkish Foreign Ministry expressed sadness over its one- sidedness and reaffirmed that recognition of Cyprus is "out of the question before a comprehensive settlement." Turkish officials insist that their ports and airports will not open to Cyprus before the isolation of northern Cyprus ends. The EU's Negotiating Framework for Turkey's accession requires Turkey to work toward normalizing relations with Cyprus and to align its position within international organizations (such as NATO) toward membership of EU member states (Cyprus) of those organizations with the policies of the EU and its member states. Cyprus has not applied to join NATO, but Turkey has blocked Cyprus from joining the Treaty on Open Skies, the Wassenaar Arrangement, the Organization of the Black Sea Economic cooperation (BSEC), and the

Lillikas. Instead, he met Speaker Christofias and Foreign Ministry officials. In the north, he met Talat, "Prime Minister" Soyer, and "Foreign Minister" Denktash.

In March 2007, U.S. Ambassador to Cyprus Ronald Schlicher encouraged representatives of the two communities to find a way to complete the work necessary for the reopening of Ledra Street. in order to stimulate broader progress on the basis of the July 8 agreement. U.S. officials repeatedly said that the United States favored implementation of the July 8 agreement.

On May 16, Under Secretary of State Nicholas Burns told a Greek-American audience that the 2004 Annan Plan was "a good effort in good faith which the U.S. supported," but "we don't need to return to something that has been tried and failed." He reported that Secretary Rice had encouraged U.N. Secretary-General Ban Ki-moon to appoint a special envoy to Cyprus.

The U.S. Embassy in Nicosia welcomed the outcome of the March 2008 Chrisofias-Talat meeting and wished them success in their efforts to reach a comprehensive settlement. The State Department vowed "full support for this constructive dialogue, and for efforts by the United Nations to forge a just and lasting Cyprus settlement." On July 28, the State Department' applauded the agreement to start direct negotiations and said that the United States was ready to support the two leaders and the U.N. process. New U.S. Ambassador to Cyprus Frank Urbancic affirmed this view when presenting his credentials to President Christofias on September 9.

Aid

On July 9, 2004, the State Department announced that $30.5 million (in reprogrammed funds) would be provided for economic development of northern Cyprus to lessen the cost of reunification. Some Members were concerned that the (Greek) Cypriot government might be bypassed. P.L. 109-102, November 14, 2005, appropriated $20 million for FY2006 as the Administration requested, providing that the funds should be made available *only* for scholarships and their administration, bicommunal projects, and measures aimed at reunification and designed to reduce tensions. This restriction pertained in each of the following years and continues in P.L. 111-8, the Omnibus Appropriations Act, 2009, signed on March 11, 2009, which provides the Administration's requested $11 million in Economic Support Funds (ESF) for Cyprus.

110TH CONGRESS LEGISLATION

S. 695, the American-Owned Property in Occupied Cyprus Claims Act. To amend the International Claims Settlement Act of 1949 to allow for claims against Turkey by U.S. nationals excluded from property they own in Turkish-occupied Cyprus. Introduced and referred to the Committee on Foreign Relations, February 27, 2007.

S.Res. 331, To express the sense of the Senate that Turkey should end its military occupation of Cyprus, particularly because Turkey's pretext has been refuted by over 13 million crossings of the divide between north and south without incident. Introduced and referred to the Committee on Foreign Relations, September 25, 2007.

H.R. 1456, introduced and referred to the House Committees on Foreign Affairs and on the Judiciary on March 9, 2007, is the same as S. 695 above.

H.Res. 405, expresses strong support for implementation of the Papadopoulos-Talat July 8, 2006 agreement. Introduced and referred to the Committee on Foreign Affairs, May 15, 2007. The Committee agreed to seek consideration under suspension of rules, September 26. The House agreed to a motion to suspend the rules and agree to the resolution, as amended, by a voice vote; motion to reconsider laid on the table and agreed to without exception on October 9.

H.Res. 407, expresses strong support for the Government of Cyprus aimed at opening additional crossing points along the cease-fire line. Introduced and referred to the Committee on Foreign Affairs, May 15, 2007.

H.Res. 620, Introduced and referred to the Committee on Foreign Affairs, August 3, 2007, is the same as S.Res. 331 above.

H.Res. 627, supporting the removal of Turkish occupation troops from the Republic of Cyprus. Introduced and referred to the Committee on Foreign Affairs, August 4, 2007.

Source: Map Resources. Adapted by CRS.

Figure 1. Map of Cyprus

End Notes

[1] Ralli Papageorgiou, "President Christofias Outlines Vision for Cyprus," Cyprus News Agency, October 7, 2008, Open Source Center Document EUP2008 1008430006.

[2] Nikolas Markantonis, "A Three-Pronged Proposal," *I Simerini*, October 28, 2008, Open Source Center Document EUP20091030142002, also Mikhalis Papadhopoulos, "The Turks want a Confederal Soluiton," *I Simerini* Online, February 28, 2009, Open Source Center Document EUP200090304 152004.

[3] "Cypriot FM: No Derogations from Acquis During a Solution," Cyprus News Agency, November 14, 2008, BBC Monitoring European, November 17, 2008.

[4] Interview with Talat by Hasan Khavecioglu,, "There Can Be No Solution Without Turkey," *Politis tis Kiriakis*, "November 2, 2008, Open Source Center Document EUP20081 103142002.

[5] Jean Christou, "Eroglu Back on the Scene with Return to UBP Head," *Cyprus Mail*, December 2, 2008.

[6] Turkey officially refers to its action as a "peace operation." The Greek Cypriots and much of the international community refer to it as an "invasion." According to the International Institute for Strategic Studies, *The Military Balance – 2009*, Turkey still has 36,000 troops on the island. However, the Greek Cypriots claim that the figure is 42,000 to 44,000. "Defense Committee: UNFICYP Figures on Occupying Troops are False," Cyprus News Agency, February 6, 2009, BBC Monitoring European.

[7] Maria Myles, "Cyprus Problem - UN Non-Paper," *CNA*, Foreign Broadcast Information Service (FBIS) Document GMP20001 109000182, November 9, 2000.

[8] "Turkey's Erdogan Faults Circles Seeking One-Sided Solutions in Cyprus," *CNN Turk*, January 3, 2003, FBIS Document GMP20030103000112.

[9] Statement made in November 20, 2003 interview published as "Cypriot President Interviewed on Cyprus Problem, EU Accession," *Politis*, November 23, 2003, FBIS Document GMP20031123000042.

[10] "Turkey: MGK Notes Need to Begin Initiatives to Revive Cyprus Negotiation Process," TRT 2 Television, FBIS Document GMP200401230001 89.

[11] Karl Vick, "Turkey Asks U.N.'s Annan to Restart Cyprus Talks," *Washington Post*, January 25, 2004.

[12] For the final Plan, see http://www.annanplan.org/.

[13] "Cyprus President Calls for Rejection of UN Reunification," BBC Monitoring European, April 8, 2004.

[14] "U.S. Accuses Greek Cypriot Leaders of Derailing Unification Vote," *New York Times*, April 27, 2004.

[15] The text of President Papadopoulos's letter to the Secretary-General is available online at http://www.antibaro.gr/ national/papadopoulos_to_anan.php.

[16] There is still a Special Representative, who is Chief of the U.N. mission and head of the U.N. Peacekeeping Force on Cyprus (UNFICYP).

[17] "Cyprus President Wants New UN Initiative for Cyprus Settlement," *CNA*, March 21, 2005, FBIS Document GMP200503222000135.

[18] For text, see http://www.mfa.gov.tr/.

[19] U.S. Embassy Nicosia Public Affairs Office, Greek Cypriot Media Reaction Report May 11, 2006, Open Source Center Document EUP2006051 1430001.

[20] See http://www.un.org/Docs/sc/ for the Secretary-General's May 23, 2006, Report on the United Nations Operation in Cyprus as well as all earlier reports and U.N. resolutions discussed below.

[21] Interview by Selim Sayari, *NTV*, date not given, Open Source Center Document GMP200708 13017001.

[22] Interview by Efi Ioannou, *Alithia*, September 10, 2007, Open Source Center Document GMP20070912430010, "Cyprus President Discusses Solution Initiatives with Turkish Cypriot Leader," *CNA*, September 11, 2007, and Jean Christou and Simon Bahceli, "Back to Square One?" *Cyprus Mail*, September 6, 2007.

[23] "Christofias: I Will Take Initiatives to Solve the Cyprus Problem," *CNA*, February 7, 2008.

[24] "I am Hopeful about a Solution, TRNC President Talat," *Anatolia*, February 25, 2008, BBC Monitoring European, February 26, 2008.

[25] Letter to the Editor, *Financial Times*, March 5, 2008.

[26] U.S. Embassy Nicosia, Public Affairs Office, Turkish Cypriot Media Reaction Report, September 12, 2006.

[27] "Military Gives Support for Cyprus Peace," *Turkish Daily News*, March 27, 2008, and "Turkish Chief of Staff says Agreement on Cyprus not Enough to Pull Out for Troops," Anatolia News Agency, March 29, 2008, BBC Monitoring European.

[28] "Erdogan Warns Against Attempts to Water Down Parameters of Cyprus Settlement," *Turkish Daily News*, July 21, 2008.

[29] Apostolis Zoupaniotis, "President Christofias Praises Ban's Interest for Cyprus Solution," *CNA*, September 22, 2008.

[30] European Union statements, official reports, and news releases may be found at http://europa.eu/.

[31] President Christofias and his AKEL party are anti-NATO and oppose applying to join the Partnership for Peace, while all other Cypriot parties favor joining.

[32] Jamie Smyth, "Turkey Takes a Further Step to EU Membership," *Irish Times*, June 13, 2006.

[33] Stavros Liyeros, "Nicosia Delineates 'Red Line,'" *I Kathimerini*, October 15, 2006, Open Source Center Document EUP20061020143003, *Turkish Daily News*, October 16, 2006.

[34] "U.S. Accuses Greek Cypriot Leaders of Derailing Unification Vote," *New York Times*, April 27, 2004.

[35] Interview conducted by Dhimitris Apokis on February 15, 2006, "The Whole Bush Administration Likes Dora," *O Kosmos tou Ependhiti*, February 25, 2006, Open Source Center Document, EUP20060227141001.

[36] Interview conducted by Anni Podhimata, *To Vima tis Kiriakis*, April 2, 2006, Open Source Center Document, EUP2006040343 1002.

[37] Speech to the 17th annual Cyprus Conference of the International Coordinating Committee - Justice for Cyprus (PSEKA) and the World Council of Hellenes (SAE).

In: Greece: Background, Debt, and Cyprus Issues ISBN: 978-1-61728-866-1
Editors: Brian D. Newmann

Chapter 5

TESTIMONY OF R. NICHOLAS BURNS, UNDER SECRETARY OF STATE, BEFORE THE HOUSE FOREIGN AFFAIRS SUBCOMMITTEE ON EUROPE, HEARING ON " U.S.-GREEK RELATIONS"*

R. Nicholas Burns

Chairman Wexler, distinguished members of the subcommittee, I thank you for allowing me to discuss a topic of great importance, one to which this Administration and the U.S. Congress are both strongly committed: the U.S.-Greece bilateral relationship. I had the privilege of serving as the United States Ambassador to Greece from 1997 to 2001, and I am proud to be among the many Philhellenes in the United States. I also want to recognize the Ambassador of the Hellenic Republic to the United States, the Honorable Alexandros Mallias, who is a dynamic advocate for U.S.-Greece relations. I thank him for his presence here today.

Let there be no doubt: Greece is a strategic Ally of the United States. As President Bush noted in his proclamation on Greek Independence Day last

* This is an edited, reformatted and augmented edition of a statement given before the United States House of Representatives Foreign Affairs Subcommittee on Europe, dated November 14, 2007.

March, "Our two nations, were both born in the belief of liberty and self-determination, sharing common cultural bonds and national values. These bonds are strengthened by a mutual commitment to democracy and freedom worldwide."

Americans helped the Greeks to win their independence from the Ottoman Empire in 1821. Americans came to Greece's aid through the Marshall Plan from 1947 to 1948. We delivered invaluable political and military assistance to Greece's democratic forces during the Greek civil war. We have been a strong ally of Greece in NATO and have admired Greece's role in the EU during the last three decades. We have stood together in every major conflict of the last century, including the World Wars, the Cold War, and the crises in Bosnia, Kosovo, and Afghanistan.

These common values and beliefs are embodied by the millions of Americans who trace their ancestry to Greece, have enriched our own country and inextricably bind our two countries. The Greek-American community is the strongest and most durable bridge linking our two countries. Greek-Americans have established hundreds of fraternal organizations that provide support services and friendship to the Greek people. They have helped to stimulate trade, investment and two-way tourism. Our Greek-American community represents American values and interests in their interactions with the Greek people. Greek-Americans are invaluable to this relationship. I could not have done my job as Ambassador without them.

As members of the Trans-Atlantic community and as NATO Allies, we work together to advance shared interests in Europe and around the world. Whether working together to stem the tide of nuclear proliferation or the trafficking of persons and illicit materials, or to protect the environment, our shared interests bring us together time and time again.

I believe that the close people-to-people ties between our two nations explain why Americans were so affected by the devastating wildfires that ravaged Greece this summer. I am confident that everyone here today can appreciate the parallels with the recent wildfires in southern California. Both events remind us that, in times of disaster, we rely on our friends and allies. I am pleased to report that the U. S. Government provided over $1.9 million in assistance to Greece, including cash donations to the Hellenic Red Cross, non-perishable commodities, and funding for a team of experts to provide technical assistance in emergency management and reconstruction. In addition to this assistance from the U.S. Government, prominent Greek-Americans and Greek-American organizations were quick to come to the aid of Greek citizens affected by the fires. Americans' generosity helped with the vital rehabilitation following this disaster. We look forward to continued, robust cooperation between Greek and American firefighters and reconstruction experts.

In the Balkans, the United States and Greece share a strong interest in ensuring that Greece's neighbors move forward on a path towards integration with NATO and the European Union. Greece's leadership and economic investment in the region have helped promote rapidly growing economies, create jobs and infrastructure, and bring a sense of stability to the region.

Greece has significant economic ties with its neighbors in the Balkans. The level of Greek investment in Albania, Serbia, including Kosovo, Montenegro, and Macedonia, reached 3.5 billion euros last year. Greece's trade relations with its neighbors are also strong. Greece has taken full advantage of new economic opportunities in the Balkans, with a new market of 50 million consumers, and has had a stable level of trade of approximately 1.5 billion euros over the last six years. Greece has also provided considerable economic assistance to its Balkan neighbors. In 2002, Greece launched a five-year aid initiative called the Hellenic Plan for Economic Reconstruction of the Balkans. This is a 700 million dollar program designed to aid the economic development of Greece's Balkan neighbors, including Albania, Bosnia-Herzogovina, Macedonia, Montenegro, Serbia and Romania.

The Balkans will require continued attention in the coming months and years to ensure a lasting peace, an ongoing economic transformation, and a permanent integration of all countries in the region into Euro-Atlantic institutions. Kosovo – the last unresolved legacy of the Milosevic regime – must see its status clarified. The United States has made this a priority for the coming months. The United States supports the EU/Russia/U.S. Troika-led negotiations as a final attempt to find a mutually agreed solution, but remains firm that its mandate will conclude on December 10.

In the absence of an agreement negotiated by December 10, the United States believes the plan for supervised independence, outlined by the UN Special Envoy Maarti Ahtisaari, is the best way forward. As a partner in NATO's Kosovo Force, Greece shares our interest in a timely resolution of this problem that maintains regional stability and ensures the rights of religious and ethnic minorities. We are working to ensure that the concerns of all parties are addressed in the negotiations now underway, but firmly believe a timely resolution of Kosovo's status must be achieved.

In the same vein, the United States and Greece share an interest in a prosperous Macedonia, one that is stable economically, politically and militarily. Macedonia has made great strides in these areas and has participated in NATO's Membership Action Plan for a number of years. This does not mean that Macedonia is guaranteed an invitation to join NATO at the Bucharest Summit this April. Our firm view is that Macedonia should be judged strictly on its merits, specifically whether it has met NATO's performance based standards.

Macedonia should not be denied an invitation to NATO for any reason other than failure to meet the substantive qualifications for entry. In Greece, some have raised the possibility of vetoing an invitation to Macedonia unless the "name issue" is resolved. While the United States agrees on the importance of resolving the name issue, we do not think that disagreement on the name alone is reason to block Macedonia's membership in international organizations.

At the same time, the name "Macedonia" is close to the heart of Greek citizens and is central and significant to the history of Greece itself. The United States is firmly committed to the UN process led by Ambassador Matt Nimetz to resolve this issue – as well as adherence to the 1995 Interim Accord, which allows Macedonia to enter regional and international organizations under the name of the Former Yugoslav Republic of Macedonia. We believe our NATO ally Greece and Macedonia are fully capable of working quietly, constructively and directly with each other and within the UN framework to reach a solution. We ask that the Macedonian government make a special effort to work with the Greek government to find a solution with which both countries can live. We ask for a spirit of compromise on both sides. The United States cannot impose a solution on either side. Finding a solution acceptable by both countries is something they need to do themselves.

It often takes considerable time for countries to join NATO. Spain didn't join until 23 years after NATO was created. It took the Baltic countries 11 years to join after their independence. But in every instance of a new member joining NATO, enlargement has benefited the Alliance and advanced peace and security in the Euro-Atlantic area. I think we all agree it is in everyone's interest to see Macedonia become a stable and cooperative neighbor of Greece and part of the NATO alliance.

Another interest that we closely share with Greece is our commitment to the diversification of energy sources and suppliers, particularly the advancement of reliable, long-term flows of oil and natural gas from the Caspian region. Energy security is inextricably linked with national security and economic prosperity. Global economic growth and stability depends on adequate, reliable and affordable supplies of energy. Greece's central position between energy producers in the Caspian and energy markets in Western

Europe means that Greece has a major role to play in helping Caspian energy find its way to a wider market.

The Turkey-Greece-Italy Interconnector (TGI) pipeline will bring Azerbaijani gas to Europe, increasing the diversity of energy supply and promoting the stability and economic prosperity of the Caspian nations. It will help to ensure that no one country will hold a monopoly on energy flows to our allies in Western and Central Europe. TGI is making solid progress. The upcoming inauguration of the Turkey-Greece portion later this month will usher in the first Azerbaijani gas exports to the EU-15. Ultimately, a trans-Adriatic link will connect the gas grids of Greece and Italy, providing a reliable flow of diversified gas supply from Azerbaijan and, potentially, other Caspian nations.

Finally, I am happy to say that we continue to cooperate closely with the Government of Greece on Greece's participation in the Visa Waiver Program. At the end of this month, the Department of Homeland Security plans to send an assessment team to Greece. The DHS team will assess Greece's readiness to participate in the Visa Waiver Program and the potential impact on U.S. security, law enforcement and immigration interests should Greece join. While this process will take some time before a decision is reached, the Government of Greece has told us that it is ready and able to meet the stringent requirements for participation. That is good news – for Greece, the United States and the business and personal ties between our two countries.

In conclusion, I want to underscore that which we treasure: the deep historical ties between the United States and Greece. We continue to work to broaden and deepen our relations. The relationship between our two countries is the best it has been in decades. We have excellent relations with Prime Minister Karamanlis and Foreign Minister Bakoyannis, and are grateful to both for their strong support of a closer U.S.-Greece alliance during their time in office. We are working together to promote peace and stability in Greece's neighborhood, the broader Middle East, and beyond. We know we can count on our Greek friends and allies to meet these challenges, and Greece can count on us.

I thank you for the opportunity to come before you today, and welcome any questions you may have.

In: Greece: Background, Debt, and Cyprus Issues ISBN: 978-1-61728-866-1
Editors: Brian D. Newmann

Chapter 6

COUNTRY ANALYSIS BRIEFS: GREECE*

Energy Information Administration

Greece has limited domestic energy resources, but it could develop into an important regional transit hub.

BACKGROUND

Greece has only minor domestic reserves of oil and gas and relies heavily on energy imports. In 2006, Greece consumed 1.4 Quadrillion Btu (Quad) of total energy of which 64 percent was petroleum followed by coal (23 percent), dry natural gas (8 percent) while hydroelectric and renewable energy combined accounted for 5 percent.

Oil consumption has increased in recent years, but has been outpaced by strong growth in demand for natural gas, driven by the development of new gas-fired power plants. The planned construction of a new oil pipeline from the Black Sea to Greece's Aegean Sea port of Alexandroupolis, the completion of a gas interconnector with Turkey, and the planned completion of a further gas link to Italy will establish the country as an important transit route for oil and gas supplies from the energy-rich Caspian Region to European markets.

* This is an edited, reformatted and augmented edition of an Energy Information Administration publication, dated February 2008.

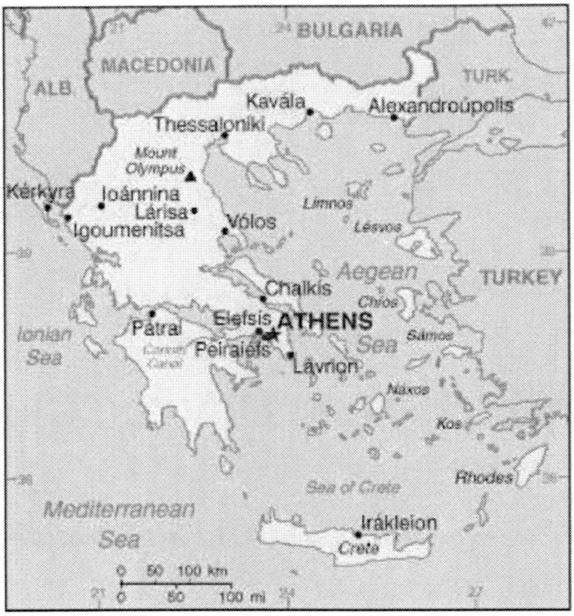

Greece Total Energy Consumption
2006

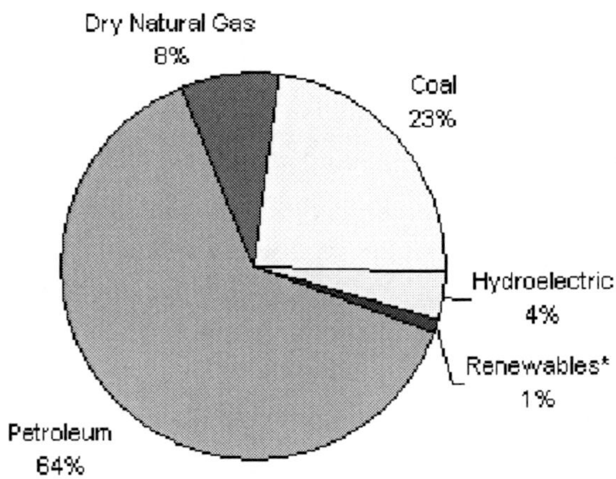

Source: EIA International Energy Annual 2006.
*Renewables include: Net Geothermal, Solar, Wind, & Wood and Waste Electric Power

OIL

Exploration and Production

As of January 1, 2009, the Oil & Gas Journal estimated Greece's oil reserves at 10 million barrels. In 2007, Greece produced 1.25 thousand barrels per day (bbl/d). Oil production comes mainly from the Prinos fields in the Aegean Sea offshore Kavala, which have been in production since 1996.

Greece has almost no domestic oil production and imports most of its oil from Iran, Saudi Arabia, Russia, Libya and Kazakhstan.

Sector Organization

Oil exploration was opened up to foreign investors through the Hydrocarbons Exploration Law No. 2289/1995. The first licensing round awarded six exploration concessions in 1996. Foreign companies are still exploring parts of the Adriatic Sea and the Black Sea, usually in conjunction with the state-controlled oil company Hellenic Petroleum (HP) or through Greek subsidiaries. Exploration and development in the Aegean Sea remains contentious due to conflicts over the continental shelf delineation between Greece and Turkey.

Hellenic Petroleum (HP) is the leader in the Greek oil market and is involved in exploration, production, and importation, along with refining, distribution and marketing. The company was formed in 1998 from former state oil company, Public Petroleum Corp. S.A. (DEP). HP manages the rights of the Greek State established under contracts with third parties on hydrocarbon exploration and production.

Consumption

Oil consumption in Greece has slowed down its rapid pace of growth rising by only approximately 10 percent between 2000 and 2007, from 400 thousand bbl/d to 438 thousand bbl/d, compared to a 35 percent increase between 1986 and 1993. Oil is the main fuel consumed by Greece, accounting for 64 percent of all energy consumption in 2006. The vast majority of

Greece's oil needs are imported, primarily from Iran, Saudi Arabia, Russia, Libya, and Kazakhstan.

Oil Pipelines

While international oil supplies are generally shipped via the Middle East or arrive through the crowded ***Bosporus*** and Dardanelles Straits near Istanbul, Greece is poised to become an important alternative transit route following the completion of the 174 mile Burgas-Alexandroupolis pipeline stretching from the Black Sea to Greece's Aegean Sea port of Alexandroupolis. A trilateral agreement between Greece, Russia and Bulgaria on construction was reached in early 2007, ending over 14 years of disagreements that delayed the project first proposed by Greece in 1994. The pipeline will provide for the export of Black Sea oil shipments on to Europe and world markets while also acting as a bypass route to the Bosporus and Dardanelles Straits.

Initial capacity will be 700,000 bbl/d of Russian and Caspian oil, potentially rising to more than 1 million barrels per day after 2016. The provisional completion date of the initial phase of the pipeline is 2009. Russia's Transneft, Rosneft, and Gazprom Neft are expected to hold equal shares, totaling a 51 percent stake in the pipeline, with the remaining 49 percent shared between Bulgaria and Greece. Kazakhstan is reportedly seeking to purchase some of the shares belonging to Greece and Bulgaria.

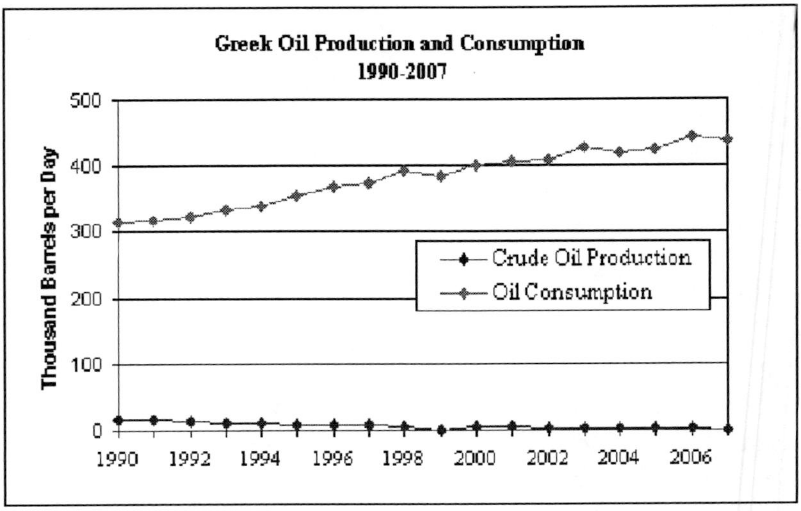

Refining and Petrochemicals

The most significant actor in the Greek refining industry is HP, which operates refineries at Aspropyrgos, Elefsina, and Thessaloniki, along with the OKTA refinery. In 2007, total refining capacity stood at 413,000 bbl/d. About two-thirds of product is sold on the inland market. Greece is largely self-sufficient in the production of lighter petroleum products, although feedstock, heating oil, and lubricants are largely imported. In the retail market, the government exercises indirect price controls by means of taxation and does retain powers to cap prices, particularly in outlying areas. Although the petroleum products market was liberalized in the early 1990s, multinationals seeking to import cheaper finished products from refineries abroad are required to hold security stocks equivalent to 25 percent of their previous year's sales. The added storage costs can often mean that imported products are effectively less competitive, and thus only specialized products are imported. HP is planning significant upgrade work at the 100,000 barrels per day Elefsina refinery, including installation of new distillate hydrocracker and coker units to raise the facility's output.

NATURAL GAS

Estimates of natural gas reserves vary, with total reserves considered to be minimal. *The Oil & Gas Journal* estimates Greek reserves to have been 70 billion cubic feet (Bcf) in January 2009. According to EIA estimates, Greek natural gas production was approximately 1 Bcf in 2007, and the country depends on Russian gas and Algerian liquefied natural gas (LNG) imports to meet its domestic demand. Gas currently constitutes a small portion of the Greek energy consumption mix, but this level is growing rapidly as the country invests in new gas-fired power plants.

Greece imports most of its natural gas from Russia but is trying to lessen its dependency by becoming a regional transit hub for natural gas from the Caspian Sea.

Sector Organization

The state-owned Public Gas Corp. (DEPA) was established in 1988 as a subsidiary of Public Petroleum Corp. S.A (DEP), to manage two gas supply contracts signed with Russia and Algeria and to operate a distribution network. DEPA is the central player in Greece's gas market, although the enactment of a new Gas Law at the end of 2005 has seen a range of market liberalization measures introduced and a greater degree of competition is now beginning to develop. The state currently has a 65 percent share in DEPA, the remaining 35 percent being held by Hellenic Petroleum.

The country's gas-distribution system is still under development. Greece has received a waiver from the European Union on gas-market liberalization, allowing it to postpone a full market opening until 2010. Retail distribution was partially privatized in 2000, when the government sold 49 percent of shareholdings and 30 year management concessions in three gas supply companies to the Italian state-controlled Italgas and to a consortium of Shell International and Cinergy of the United States.

Greece Dry Natural Gas Production and Consumption (1990-2006)

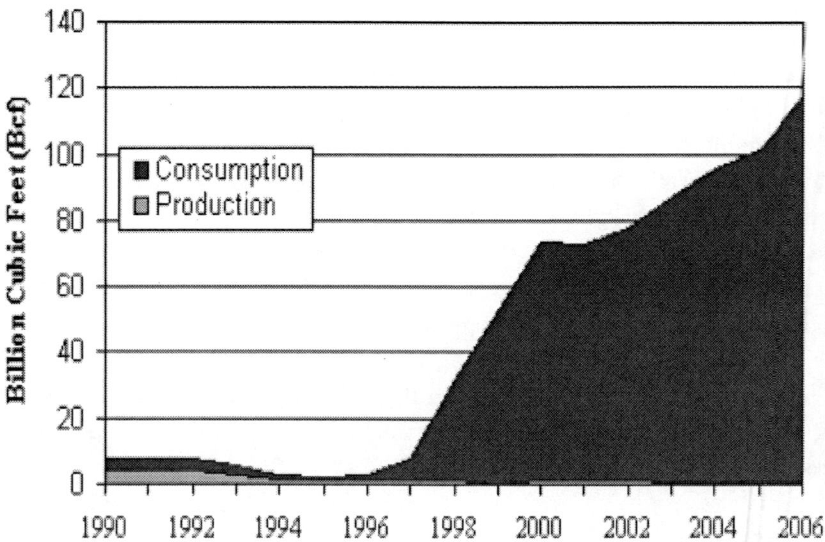

Consumption

Natural gas consumption has steadily increased over the past 20 years, jumping by over 78 percent between 1996 and 2006 to 17 Bcf. While the rate of growth of consumption may decline from these highs, gas consumption will continue to grow steadily as new gas-fired power plants are installed. Annual demand growth is expected to average 2.8 percent between 2010 and 2030 according to EIA estimates.

Natural Gas Pipelines

Greece has been developing its natural gas network since 1997, importing from Russia via pipeline and Algeria in liquefied form. Greece is being positioned as a potential regional gas hub and a transit route for the delivery of Central Asian and Russian gas supplies to Europe. A 186-mile interconnector passing under the Sea of Marmara linking the Greek and Turkish gas grids came onstream in 2007. A further extension via the 372-mile Turkey-Greece-Italy interconnectors across northern Greece and the 136-mile Trans-Adriatic pipeline under the Adriatic Sea to Italy is to be built by 2011, paving the way for supplies from Azerbaijan's giant Shah Deniz gas field in the Caspian Sea to be delivered via Greece to Europe. Following the completion of the Turkey-Greece interconnector, Greece began receiving gas from Azerbaijan, although these supplies were halted at the beginning of 2008 following disruptions caused by a dispute between Turkmenistan and Iran. Azerbaijani imports will likely increase as the Turkey- Greece interconnector is further utilized.

Greece also continues to import a substantial proportion of its supplies from Russia and recently signed on to the Gazprom-led South Stream gas pipeline project in April 2008. Greek DEPA purchases 98 Bcf of its supplies from Russia's Gazexport, a subsidiary of Gazprom. Imports from Russia account for 75 percent of Greece's needs with Algerian LNG providing most of the remainder.

In January 2008 DEPA and the Italian Edison company signed a letter of intent which established Poseidon SA, a company that will own and operate the Poseidon sub-sea gas pipeline. The 131-mile long pipeline will have a capacity of 282 Bcf. Initially natural gas will come from the Caspian Sea, via Azerbaijan and Turkey by the end of 2012, when it is expected to be completed. DEPA and Edison each have a 50 percent share in the Poseidon pipeline which will run from the Greek port of Stavrolimenas in northwest Greece, to Otranto in southeast Italy.

Other projects that aim to transport Caspian gas to Italy are a pipeline from western Turkey to the Greek town of Komotini, and a 186-mile link connecting Greece's gas pipeline network with Stavrolimenas. The latter is being built at DEPA's expense.

Liquefied Natural Gas (LNG)

Greece has one LNG import terminal situated at Revithoussa on mainland Greece, west of Athens. Supplies are imported under a contract with Algeria's Sonatrach. Kavala, in northern Greece, has also been considered as a site for a new LNG terminal.

ELECTRICITY

Greece's geography has led to the development of a fragmented electricity system, with less than half of the country's power plants connected to the mainland grid. The majority of power plants are in the north where the lignite fields are located, while the bulk of demand is in and around the region of Attica in the south, where 40 percent of the popoulation and most of the country's industry reside. Interconnection between the country's numerous islands remains low, albeit increasing. Domestic lignite remains the most important fuel for electricity generation, although the use of natural gas is growing rapidly and renewable energy use is also expected to expand. The total system consists of some 12,800 megawtts (MW) of installed capacity with a further 850 MW of interconnectors for imports.

Greece will likely benefit from greater electricity connections with its neighbors.

Sector Organization

Although Greece has liberalized its electricity sector, former state monopoly Public Power Corporation (PPC) continues to hold a dominant position. PPC's effective monopoly has seen prices capped, and power tariffs remain below European Union (EU) averages. It currently operates around 96 percent of all generation, although competition is developing quickly and recently there has been entry of several European power companies to the market, often in partnership with a Greek firm. Transmission services are run by Hellenic Transmission System Operator (HTSO), in which PPC holds a 49 percent stake.

Coal

In 2006, coal represented a 23 percent share of Greece's total energy consumption, the second largest share after petroleum. Lignite, or brown coal is Greece's only significant fossil fuel resource, with total recoverable reserves totaling approximately 4,300 million short tons (Mmst). Greece is second only to Germany in the EU for lignite coal production and the largest deposits are at Ptolemais and Amintaio in Northern Greece. Since Greece has no hard coal reserves, it is imported from South Africa, Russia, Venezuela and Colombia. Domestic production has been partly opened to private companies, but the Public Power Corporation (PPC) remains the largest producer and holds the right to over 90 percent of Greece's production licenses.

Renewable Energy

Hyrdoelectricity combined with other renewables including geothermal, solar, wind, wood and waste electric power comprised 5 percent of Greece's total energy balance in 2006. By EU mandate 20 percent of Greece's electricity production must be generated by renewables by 2010. Greece has developed wind parks with installed capacity of roughly 650 MW.

PROFILE

Energy Overview

Proven Oil Reserves (January 1, 2009)	10 million barrels
Oil Production (2007)	1,250 barrels per day
Oil Consumption (2007)	438 thousand barrels per day
Crude Oil Distillation Capacity (2009)	423 thousand barrels per day
Proven Natural Gas Reserves (January 1, 2009)	70 billion cubic feet
Natural Gas Production (2007E)	1 billion cubic feet
Natural Gas Consumption (2007E)	144 billion cubic feet
Recoverable Coal Reserves (2005)	4,299 million short tons
Coal Production (2007E)	73 million short tons
Coal Consumption (2007E)	75 million short tons
Electricity Installed Capacity (2007E)	13 gigawatts
Electricity Production (2007E)	59 billion kilowatt hours
Electricity Consumption (2006E)	56 billion kilowatt hours
Total Energy Consumption (2006)	1.42 quadrillion Btus*, of which Oil (64%), Coal (23%), Natural Gas (8%), Hydroelectricity (4%), Other Renewables (1%), Nuclear (0%)
Total Per Capita Energy Consumption (2006)	139 million Btus
Energy Intensity (2006)	5,684 Btu per $2000-PPP**

Environmental Overview

Energy-Related Carbon Dioxide Emissions (2006)	107 million metric tons, of which Oil (62%), Coal (33%), Natural Gas (6%)
Per-Capita, Energy-Related Carbon Dioxide Emissions (2006)	10 metric tons
Carbon Dioxide Intensity (2006)	0.4 Metric tons per thousand $2000-PPP**

Oil and Gas Industry

Organization	Partially-privatized
Foreign Company Involvement	BOTAS (Turkey), GN (Spain), Sonatrach (Algeria), Gazprom (Russia)
Major Oil Fields	Prinos, Kallirachi
Major Oil and Gas Ports	Alexandoupolis, Reuithoussa, Thessaloniki
Major Pipelines	South Caucasus Pipeline; Turkey-Greece pipeline; Poseidon pipeline
Major Refineries	Aspropyrgos (135,500 bbl/d), Elefsis (100,000 bbl/d), Thessaloniki (67,000 bbl/d)

* The total energy consumption statistic includes petroleum, dry natural gas, coal, net hydro, nuclear, geothermal, solar, wind, wood and waste electric power.

** GDP figures from Global Insight estimates based on purchasing power parity (PPP) exchange rates.

Links

EIA Links

EIA Data for Greece
CIA World Factbook, Greece
U.S. Department of Energy's Office of
U.S. Department of State Consular Information Sheet, Greece
Centre For Renewable Energy Sources (CRES)
EarthTrends: Greece Country Profile
Greece.com: Government
Greek Connection
Helapco: Hellenic Association of Photovoltaic Companies
Hellenic Petroleum (HP)
Motor Oil (Hellas)

Sources

Agence -France Presse
CIA World Factbook
Dow Jones News wire service
Economist Intelligence Unit ViewsWire

Financial Times
Global Insight
Oil and Gas Journal
Petroleum Economist
International Market Insight Reports
Global Power Report
Reuters
National Trade Data Bank
Petroleum Intelligence Weekly
Platt's Oilgram News
U.S. Energy Information Administration
World Gas Intelligence
World Markets Energy

INDEX

F

G

M

N

O

P

Q

R